Cultural Diversity and Inclusive Teaching

Shibao Guo
Zenobia Jamal

London, Canada

**STLHE
SAPES**

Society for Teaching and Learning in Higher Education
La société pour l'avancement de la pédagogie dans
l'enseignement supérieur

STLHE Green Guides

Series Editor:
Alan Wright,
University of Windsor

Editorial Assistant:
Beverley Hamilton,
University of Windsor

Founding Series Editor:
Christopher Knapper,
Queen's University

Associate Series Editors:
Carol O'Neil,
Dalhousie University

Eileen Herteis,
Mount Allison University

Roger Moore,
St. Thomas University

International Associate
Series Editor:
David Jaques,
Oxford, U.K.

Editorial Board Members:
John Thompson, University of Saskatchewan; Nicola Simmons, Brock University; Maureen Wideman, University of Ontario Institute of Technology; Jeanette McDonald, Wilfrid Laurier University; Paula Brook, University of Alberta; Rosalie Pedersen, University of Calgary; Pamela Miller, University of Calgary; Alice MacPherson, Kwantlen University College

Publishing Co-ordinator:
Debra Dawson,
Teaching Support Centre,
The University of Western Ontario

Director of Retail Services
Steve Alb, The Book Store at Western,
The University of Western Ontario

Distributed on behalf of STLHE by:
The Book Store at Western,
University Community Centre,
The University of Western Ontario,
London, Ontario N6A 3K7

Library and Archives Canada Cataloguing in Publication
Guo, Shibao, 1965-
    Cultural diversity and inclusive teaching / Shibao Guo & Zenobia Jamal

(Green Guide, No. 8)
Includes bibliographical references and index.
ISSN 1718-2115   ISBN 978-0-9738227-3-1

1. Multicultural education–Canada. 2. Minorities in higher education–Canada. 3. Pluralism (Social sciences)–Study and teaching (Higher)–Canada. 4. Education, Higher–Social aspects–Canada. I. Jamal, Zenobia, 1957- II. Society for Teaching and Learning in Higher Education. III. Title. IV. Series: Green guide (Society for Teaching and Learning in Higher Education).

LC1200.G86 2007   378'.0170971   C2007-903163-3

Cite as:
Guo, Shibao and Jamal, Zenobia (2007). Cultural Diversity and Inclusive Teaching. London, ON: Society for Teaching and Learning in Higher Education

Foreword

We are pleased to present *Cultural Diversity and Inclusive Practice*, the eighth in the Green Guide Series of the Society for Teaching and Learning in Higher Education. Thoroughly grounded in educational research and the writers' lived experience, the Green Guides offer practical approaches to the many challenges and opportunities facing instructors in post-secondary classrooms. In this Guide, Shibao Guo and Zenobia Jamal bring you the fruit of their many years' experience engaging with the complexity of culturally diverse groups in classrooms, and of their life experience as both students and instructors negotiating cross-culturally in teaching and learning. The Guide emerges out of their understanding of the importance of being open to difference, both its challenge and its rich potential in the classroom, and explores this basic premise as a matter of principle, of mindset, and of practice, through strategies for fostering environments more open to cultural diversity.

The STLHE Green Guide series was originally patterned after a successful series produced by our colleagues in the Higher Education and Research Development Society of Australasia (HERDSA). They have published similar guides since 1984. HERDSA generously allowed us to adopt their title for our own series and Christopher Knapper, the Founding Series Editor, introduced the idea to Canada in 1998. Since then, STLHE has sold thousands of copies of the Guides across Canada, and they are in regular use on campuses throughout the country and internationally. The series' use of clear, jargon-free language, its practical approach, and its accessibility have made the Guides popular and effective tools in fostering active and engaged learning on post-secondary campuses.

We would like, especially, to thank the peer reviewers and this guide's editor, Alice MacPherson (Kwantlen University College), for their commitment to the series and the many voluntary hours they have put into the development of this Guide. Since its inception, the Green Guide series has been the labour of authors, editors, and referees who freely donate their time to this Society for Teaching and Learning in Higher Education initiative. It is their effort that makes the continuation of this successful series affordable and possible.

Alan Wright
Series Editor

Beverley Hamilton
Editorial Assistant

Teaching Journeys: Introducing the Authors

Interviews and Preface by Beverley Hamilton and Alan Wright

The life stories of this Green Guide's authors, based on their own words and narratives, offer a glimpse into their lived experience and life-long commitment to promoting culturally inclusive learning environments.

Shibao Guo

Born in Shandong province, China, Shibao "caught the tail end of the Cultural Revolution" and, in keeping with the educational policies of this period, his school emphasized community learning. He and his classmates spent much of their time in the countryside, working with and learning from labourers and factory workers. For Shibao, these experiences placed school in a broad social context. Despite its adherence to Mao's call for "Learning by Practice" (Guo, 2004), however, Shibao describes his education as still strongly influenced by Confucian principles. Even these early experiences resonate with complex, culturally informed tensions.

Shibao's university education took place as China's adoption of pragmatism ushered in a period of intense social change. He studied English Language and Literature at Shandong Normal University and subsequently worked in the University's International Exchange Programs office as an interpreter and coordinator of student and instructor exchanges. Working with international instructors fostered his growing interest in how people's diverse cultural backgrounds shaped profoundly different approaches to teaching and learning, and culturally distinctive interaction styles between learners and teachers. Shibao was offered a scholarship to pursue graduate education at the

The English accent was a big challenge for me, and also the learning environment....Another difficulty I had was...making connections in terms of the content I learned in both Canada and the UK. The content tended to be very North American or Eurocentric.... Sometimes I feel [it's] very irrelevant to where you came from. Certainly, when I began to teach, I tried to make the effort in building more inclusive teaching strategies, and selecting materials from all sorts of different backgrounds.

Shibao

University of Nottingham (UK), where his research involved a comparative study of adult teaching and learning in China and the United Kingdom.

Despite the fact that he had worked with many of the professors in the program when he was still in China, and had studied English and used the language professionally for many years, living, studying, and working in an unfamiliar culture involved a steep learning curve. It was more than a language issue: there was the issue of accent to contend with, and the nature and expectations of the learning environment, where he often found it difficult to make meaning from the culturally specific references in classroom and extracurricular interaction.

Shibao moved to Canada in 1993, where he first lived in Regina and then moved to Vancouver to complete his doctoral work at the University of British Columbia (UBC). There he grew interested in the issues of citizenship and immigration in Canada, and in the complexities of how cultural diversity is embedded within cultures of teaching

> *In terms of cultural diversity,...people are afraid of saying the wrong thing, doing the wrong thing, and so people tend to avoid dealing with it. So, bringing that issue to the forefront is very important.*
>
> **Shibao**

and learning. He applied his expertise in adult education to his work at UBC's Teaching and Academic Growth Centre and also at the Centre for Intercultural Communication, where, among other activities, he facilitated professional development courses for international teaching and research assistants. He also taught undergraduate teacher education courses focusing on issues of social justice and equity. He was an Assistant Professor in the Department of Educational Policy Studies at the University of Alberta. He now teaches at the University of Calgary, where he is currently cross-appointed to the Graduate and Teacher Education divisions. Shibao specializes in workplace and adult learning, but has also continued to teach foundational courses in Education and Society as well as courses on Adult Education. His wide-ranging research activities explore immigrant settlement experience and services, Chinese diaspora, international graduate teaching assistant development, and Chinese educational philosophy.

Zenobia Jamal

Zenobia was born in Kenya. Her grandparents migrated there from India, and she remembers the African social context there as a "pretty diverse environment." When she began her education, some ten years after Kenya gained its independence, schools still followed what was effectively a British curriculum, and were run primarily by British expatriates. As she grew older, Kenyan schools began to emphasize indigenous and local knowledge to a greater degree, and required, for example, the study of Swahili and of African literature. Many more Kenyan teachers were hired. Like Shibao, Zenobia's early educational experiences were a powerful introduction into the culturally constructed and shifting nature of learning environments.

When her family moved to Vancouver in the mid-seventies, Zenobia was just completing secondary school. She attended UBC, graduating with a degree in Computer Science. Thinking back to those years, she remembers being "very mystified" by references to cultural knowledge to which she had little direct access. In retrospect, Zenobia has come to understand that the combined processes of migration and entering university made her undergraduate career more difficult. She believes that more consciously and carefully constructed learning environments can make university learning a much more accessible and positive experience for culturally diverse students.

Over the next fifteen years, Zenobia worked in information technology, raised a family,

When I first arrived in Canada and I started my undergrad degree at UBC, I remember being very mystified – actually all the way through my program – by so many of the cultural references, a whole set of knowledge that I had no access to, about even just the whole process of education, just the terminology that was used, even the way the courses were structured. So there were things I just didn't get for a long time. It was just taken for granted that everybody had this system, everybody understood the system. I almost needed a broker, someone that I could go and ask, and initially it was very hard, because people would look at you – what are you asking, you don't know that? When that's accompanied by a whole process of migration which is difficult enough…I didn't realize how difficult it was until…I looked back. But my experience could have been very different had I been in learning environments that were different.

Zenobia

and became increasingly engaged in community-based learning. She worked with immigrant youth, in family education, with parenting groups, and with individuals negotiating the settlement process. In these roles, she has acted as the kind of 'broker' she remembers needing as a recently arrived university student. In an effort to design learning environments that met the needs of these very diverse groups, she began to explore different pedagogical practices. Zenobia's interest in creating these learning environments has become a consistent thread in her life and work, and in the year 2000 she returned to school, ultimately to pursue graduate studies in Adult Education. With a partner, she also runs a company that develops workshops on cultural diversity in the workplace, encouraging individuals to examine the many kinds of difference they encounter in the workplace, and providing theory

and strategies for working across difference in productive and equitable ways. Zenobia's current research on the informal and formal learning experiences of immigrant women during migration and settlement examines the kinds of programs that best meet their needs once they arrive in Canada. She has also taken part in research on the role of service organizations as spaces where newcomers re-negotiate identities and forge new conceptions of community, and on the complexities of difference in the workplace.

Over the years I worked with...diverse groups with different experiences. I worked with immigrant youths, and did some family life education, parenting groups—how do you create these learning environments, what do you have to do differently to meet the needs of these learners? Experimenting, different pedagogical practices to come up with things that would meet [their] needs...and I think that...was kind of a thread over many years.

Zenobia

Writing the Green Guide

This Green Guide grew out of Zenobia and Shibao's separate experiences of migration, settlement, learning, and teaching in diverse settings, and out of their deep commitment to constructing and promoting inclusive and equitable learning environments. Their varied expertise, scholarship, and instructional experience serve as the foundation for the balance of theoretical information and

practical strategies contained within its pages. Two elements, in particular, recur in their stories and goals: encouraging people to overcome their fear of dealing with difference and encouraging them to construct environments that foster a sense of community membership for all. It is the authors' hope that this guide will encourage people to see difference as a locus of opportunity and richness as well as challenge, especially given the increasingly diverse nature of higher education settings in Canada.

There's a fear of diversity, so we tend to focus on the sameness, on what are our similarities and commonalities, in the hope that that will bring people together and...will create environments... suitable for many different kinds of people. But I think when we ignore difference, there's the danger that there are many aspects of individuals that we negate or we don't validate.... Acknowledging it and learning how to be open to it.... It's something we need to emphasize and to work at.

Zenobia

Experiences of diversity in learning environments have fostered in both of these teachers and researchers a sense of the importance of inclusive citizenship, where difference and belonging are compatible and desirable qualities. For both of them, the growth of such communities is a central tenet of learning in a democratic, equitable, and just society. It is their hope that the guide will offer practical strategies, but even more, that it will inspire you to think more deeply about diversity, to talk about it, and to explore and work with others to build inclusive environments suitable to your learners' needs. They hope this guide enriches your teaching, your students' opportunities, and the learning communities that you build together.

The belonging part of citizenship is very important...both for newly arrived immigrants and also for visible minority students in university settings – creating a community where everybody feels they belong is a very important part of inclusive citizenship.

Shibao

Contents

Acknowledgements

The completion of this Green Guide would have been impossible without the support and help of many individuals. Here, we can only mention some of them by name. First and foremost, we are indebted to the Editorial team for their time and effort in making this Guide "a first-rate manuscript." We would like to give special thanks to Alan Wright and Alice Macpherson for working with us closely in developing this Green Guide. The anonymous reviewers provided insightful comments and suggestions, which we are thankful for. The idea of developing this Green Guide was initiated in a conversation with Christopher Knapper at an orientation workshop for new faculty members at the University of Alberta. We would like to thank Christopher for his initial encouragement and helpful suggestions.

Our gratitude and appreciation also go to our colleagues, workshop participants, and students who enriched our understanding of and experience with teaching, learning, and cultural diversity: Gary Poole, Gail Riddell, Alice Cassidy, Janice Johnson, Ingrid Price, Desiree Mou, Jennifer Jasper, and Catherine Bennington at the Centre for Teaching and Academic Growth (TAG), the University of British Columbia (UBC); Mackie Chase, Allan English, Karen Rolston, and Pat Marshall at the Centre for Intercultural Communication, UBC; Tara Fenwick, Katy Campbell, Tara Gibb, and Evelyn Hamdon at the University of Alberta; Edmund Dale at the University of Regina; John Daines, Brian Graham, Sue Dobson, and Andy Dobson in the United Kingdom.

Last, we would like to express our heartfelt thanks to our families for their love, support, and inspiration: Edmund and Yan Guo (who also helped us with the initial book proposal); Tariq, Khalid, Aliya, and Iqbal Jamal. We could not have done it without you.

Introduction

Canadian universities and colleges are becoming increasingly ethnoculturally diverse. Two major social forces have contributed to this change: immigration and increasing enrolment of international students. Minority and international students bring their values, language, culture, and educational background to our campuses, adding to the richness of our educational environments. To build an inclusive campus we have the ethical and educational responsibility to embrace such difference and diversity and to integrate it into all aspects of university life, including teaching and learning, administration, counseling, and student services. Cultural diversity has the potential to contribute to a richer learning environment but we still face many challenges every day. One of the most important of these is a fear of diversity, partly resulting from a lack of knowledge and readiness to approach diversity (Palmer, 1998).

The goal of this Green Guide is to examine common approaches to embracing cultural diversity in higher education, particularly for the purpose of enhancing teaching and learning. The Guide addresses the following topics:

- the magnitude of cultural diversity in Canadian higher education

- challenges facing educators in a diverse society

- current models used to address diversity

- strategies for developing inclusive pedagogical practices.

This Guide is organized into five chapters. The first maps the demographics of diversity in higher education, provides definitions of cultural diversity, and examines some issues that arise in dealing with cultural diversity. The second reviews three models addressing cultural diversity, used to develop inclusive teaching strategies. Chapter three describes the factors that influence the teaching and learning environment. Chapter four of the Guide suggests strategies that can be used to respond to culturally diverse students. The final chapter offers further strategies for teaching linguistically diverse students. We hope that instructors, instructional designers, student counselors, and administrators will find this Guide helpful.

1. Mapping Diversity in Higher Education

Diversity in Higher Education

Canada is a society of immigrants. Immigration played an important role in establishing Canada as an ethnoculturally diverse and economically prosperous nation. The 2001 Census reveals that as of May 15, 2001, 18.4 percent of the total population was born outside Canada, and that 13.4 percent were visible minorities compared with 4.7 percent in 1981 (Statistics Canada, 2003a). A large proportion of the recent immigrants to Canada came from Asia, the Middle East, the Caribbean, Central and South America, and Africa. Furthermore, according to the Ethnic Diversity Survey (Statistics Canada, 2003b), almost one-quarter (23 percent) of Canada's total population of 22.4 million people aged 15 years and older were first-generation Canadians: that is, they were born outside Canada. The latter number indicates that a large proportion of the new immigrants are university age students who are 18 years and older.

Changing demographics have subsequently transformed the student population in higher education. According to the 2001 Canadian Undergraduate Survey Consortium (AUCC, 2002), about 15 percent of first-year students self-identified as visible minorities. Furthermore, Canadian university and college campuses host a significant number of international students. According to the OECD Annual Report (2003), 70,000 new international students registered in Canada in 2001 (about 10,000 more than in 2000), which brings the total to nearly 137,000 in contrast to 37,000 in 1980. At the graduate level, international students accounted for 17 percent of the total student body; these students play an important role in producing and disseminating knowledge in Canadian universities.

Without a doubt, these changes have created new opportunities for development as well as new challenges. In particular, we are left grappling with questions, such as: What are the implications of such profound social and demographic changes for teaching and learning in higher education? Are our universities and colleges, as well as our instructors, ready for such changes? Do our curricula and teaching approaches reflect such diversity?

Defining Cultural Diversity

To understand the impact of diversity in the educational setting, it is first necessary to define some key terms, including culture and cultural diversity. Culture can be defined as a dynamic system of values, beliefs, and behaviours that influence how people experience and respond to the world around them. Marshall (2002) defines cultural diversity as "distinctions in the lived experiences, and the related perceptions of and reactions to those experiences, that serve to differentiate collective populations from one another" (p. 7). Although cultural groups share commonalties in perspectives, behaviours and ways of being in the world, they are rarely homogenous. Within each cultural group, there are differences that affect the way individual members in the group relate to one another and to the group as a whole. Although aspects of culture such as race and ethnicity are more visible, differences within groups such as class and gender intersect and affect other aspects of individual identity and group membership. Members of one cultural group may simultaneously belong to several groups, and these multiple group memberships result in aspects of identity that respond to, conflict with, and contradict each other as individuals grow and develop. Culture, therefore, cannot be viewed as an organizing principle that creates static borders based on race or ethnicity; it is constantly changing, dynamic, and fluid (Ghosh & Abdi, 2004; Claxton, Pollard & Sutherland, 2003; McLaren, 2003).

Culture and education are inextricably intertwined, and students' perspectives and worldviews influence their experiences in educational environments (Adams, 1992; Gay, 2000; Jones, 2004; Wlodkowski & Ginsberg, 1995). Culture plays a part in shaping the ways in which students learn and communicate, how they relate to other students and instructors, their motivation levels, and their sense of what is worth learning. The degree to which students feel comfortable in the learning environment will depend on the congruence between their cultural background and the dominant culture of the educational institution. It is important, therefore, that educators "become aware of the ways in which the traditional classroom culture excludes or constrains learning for some students and learn how to create environments that acknowledge the cultural diversity that new students bring" (Adams, 1992, p. 7). While this Guide focuses on immigrant and international students, it is important to remember those visible minority students who were born in Canada and speak fluent English, and who face challenges because of their ethnic and cultural background.

In addition to the responsibility that institutions of higher education have in meeting the needs of diverse students, there is evidence that increased diversity in higher education can benefit students from all backgrounds, both from majority as well as from minority groups (Casteneda, 2004). These benefits include an improvement in intergroup relations and campus climate, increased opportunities for accessing support and mentoring systems, opportunities for acquiring broader perspectives and viewpoints, and participation in complex discussions, all of which can contribute to increased learning. Cultural diversity can be seen as strength and as a resource fostering an empowering environment for all students.

Issues in Dealing with Cultural Diversity

Although the goal of responding to cultural diversity and providing an environment in which it can flourish is a lofty one, there are several issues to consider. These include identifying varying perspectives on difference and diversity, resistance to the focus on cultural diversity, and issues of knowledge construction and validation.

Efforts to implement diversity initiatives within educational institutions are often met with avoidance of the issue, or denial of the necessity of responding to diversity. The 'colourblind perspective' sees cultural, racial, and ethnic background as irrelevant, and assumes that treating all individuals the same will erase issues of inequity and injustice (Solomon & Levine-Rasky, 2003). Although this view is superficially appealing, because it seems to value all individuals equally, it negates the histories, backgrounds, and experiences of diverse cultural groups, and ignores the ways in which these affect their experiences in the learning environment. Colourblind policies which endeavor to treat all students the same may end up contributing to the perpetuation of injustices (Ghosh & Abdi, 2004). In contrast, educators must be colour sensitive to affirm and validate difference rather than minimize it, striving to gain a fuller understanding of their students.

The notion of diversity is linked to the way in which difference is perceived. Difference is not implicitly problematic; its consequences are contingent on the way people perceive and respond to it (Banks, 1997a). People often view difference relative to the dominant norm as a negative, leading to the use of the 'difference as deficit' model. The deficit model views difference as something that needs to be dealt with and corrected, leading to inequitable educational practices. Teachers operating with this perspective ignore or minimize diversity, and view attending to difference as a hindrance and an obstacle to the learning process (Vasques-Scalera, 2002). They do not see diversity as an opportunity to enhance learning by using the diverse strengths, experiences, knowledge, and perspectives of students from various cultural groups. The 'essentialist' approach to difference is one in which the individual ascribes a fixed set of characteristics and uses those characteristics to predict or explain behaviour (Woodward, 1997). This approach ignores differences within groups and can lead to incorrect or even harmful stereotypes. When applied to an educational setting, both the 'difference as deficit' and the 'essentialist' approaches to difference can lead to inequitable pedagogical practices.

The primary task of higher education is the construction, generation, and dissemination of knowledge. However, typically, the dominant group determines what constitutes valid knowledge, resulting in a Eurocentric curriculum that primarily reflects the perspectives, standards, and values of this group and ignores the knowledge and experiences of non-European minority groups (Dei, James, Karumanchery, James-Wilson & Zine, 2000; Kitano, 1997a; Tisdell, 1995). This situation conveys the message that the construction of knowledge is restricted to those who have the power to validate and affirm it. Responding to a culturally diverse student population requires educators to transform the curriculum to include multiple ways of knowing, centering previously marginalized knowledge.

2. Responding to Cultural Diversity: A Review of Selected Models

Spheres of Influence

The literature on responding to diversity within educational settings provides a rich array of frameworks and models that can be used as starting points to explore and understand the roles faculty can play. Kitano (1997a) identifies several spheres of influence through which faculty can promote equity within an organization. These spheres of influence include the self, classroom, institution, and community (See Figure 1).

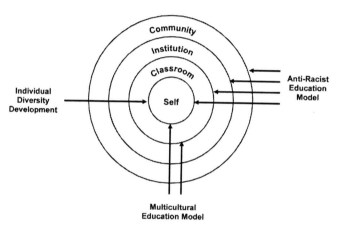

Figure 1: Spheres of Influence
Adapted from Kitano (1997a)

Gay (2000) suggests that, in order for educators to become culturally responsive, they need first to learn about the relationship between cultural diversity and education. Educators must also become more aware of the values, beliefs, and attitudes that affect how they perceive and respond to diversity since these will affect the quality of their interaction with students.

The first model we present is an intercultural education model for the development of individual diversity. Professionals in higher education can use the model to reflect on their own attitudes towards diversity, and to promote and influence the attitudes of students and other members of the campus community towards cultural diversity (Chávez, Guido-DiBrito & Mallory, 2003). The second is a multicultural education model (Banks, 1997a; Banks, 1997b) that provides a framework for curriculum change and reform which can be applied at the level of the individual and the classroom. Third, we include a critical integrative framework for inclusive education, modeled on an anti-racist approach to education (Dei, James-Wilson & Zine, 2001). This framework is based on the assumption that education can play a role in promoting social justice and equity, and operates at all four levels of influence: the self, classroom, institution, and community.

Intercultural Education

The goal of the intercultural education movement of the 1920s and 1930s was to promote tolerance and understanding between different cultural and ethnic groups, and this movement spurred efforts within the educational system and the community to respond to cultural diversity (Banks, 2005). It was based on the assumptions that similarities between groups were more important than differences, and that having enough information about cultural groups would avert prejudice and bias and promote respect and acceptance. The movement provided the impetus for programs that would help increase knowledge of other cultures, develop positive attitudes towards difference, and teach the skills of interacting and communicating across difference. This could be done through the acquisition of intercultural competencies, defined as, the "long-term change of a person's knowledge (cognition), attitudes (emotions), and skills (behaviour) to enable positive and effective interaction with members of other cultures" (Otten, 2003, p. 15). The 1960s and the 1970s saw the rise of the multicultural education movement which retained many of the initial goals of the intercultural education movement.

The intercultural education movement has affected efforts to address cultural diversity in higher education that focus on creating changes in attitudes in order to create more equitable teaching and learning environments. Instructors and students both come to the teaching environment with varied experiences and social and cultural backgrounds, and may operate from unexamined assumptions about the characteristics of cultural groups with whom they are unfamiliar (Marchesani & Adams, 1992). These assumptions are often part of mainstream cultural knowledge and, unless questioned and challenged, can become the basis from which individuals interact with minority cultural groups. In addition, teachers and students often incorrectly apply information about general group characteristics to their interactions with individuals. Reflecting on and challenging assumptions requires change at the individual level.

An Intercultural Education Model

Although learning about other cultures and developing intercultural competencies is an important starting point in efforts to respond to cultural diversity, a sole focus on this goal runs the risk of defining differences in terms of cultural group membership, when in fact these are mediated by many other factors such as social and historical contexts and personal experiences in these contexts. A more useful response to cultural diversity is to understand the complex identities of individuals, rather than seeing them as members of a cultural group with a fixed set of characteristics.

The Individual Diversity Development Framework is one of the intercultural models used to address attitudes towards cultural diversity in educational settings. Proposed by Chávez et al. (2003), it provides a holistic approach for cognitive, affective, and behavioral transformation, and can be used to guide students, staff, and faculty reflection on their own development and to encourage and assist in the development of others. As noted above, individuals often use an essentialist approach to understand cultural difference rather than acknowledge the complex and sometimes contradictory nature of identity; individuals are members of many different groups, making it difficult to understand them through one set of characteristics. The Individual Diversity Development Framework demonstrates how individuals can gain a deeper understanding of the complexity of identities, and move towards valuing and validating these complexities. This change usually occurs at three levels – first at the cognitive level, followed by the affective and behavioural levels. The change may not be linear, and will occur gradually through practice. In fact, individuals may shift from one dimension to another depending on context and situation. The Individual Diversity Development Framework has five dimensions: lack of exposure to the other, dualistic awareness, questioning and self-exploration, risk-taking, and integration (see Table 1); learning to value a certain kind of difference can occur by moving through some or all of these dimensions.

Unawareness or Lack of Exposure to the Other

In this first dimension, individuals may be cognitively unaware of a certain kind of difference, exhibit no feeling about this difference, and in their behaviour show no response to the difference. This could be due to a lack of exposure: for example, young children are often unaware of differences in skin colour. Given the increased diversity of educational institutions, it is unlikely that many individuals would be at this stage of awareness. However, there may be some differences that are less apparent, and individuals at this level can benefit from activities encouraging them to reflect on differences that they are familiar with in order to move them towards a consideration of other less familiar kinds of differences such as cultural diversity.

Dualistic Awareness

Individuals operating within this dimension see difference in a dualistic way, as valuing similarity and denigrating that which is different. They may choose to ignore or avoid contact with difference, or try to minimize the differences they encounter. These individuals may not have had their beliefs questioned or challenged. Activities that can assist individuals in this dimension expose them to varied perspectives on issues in order to move them away from dualistic modes of thinking. For example, teachers could ask individuals or groups to take a stand on a particular issue, and then ask them to consider the opposing opinions or arguments on the issue. These activities should include an explicitly affective element, since merely having knowledge of difference does not necessarily lead to valuing difference.

Table 1

A Framework of Individual Diversity Development

Dimension	Description	Cognitive	Affective	Behavioural
Lack of Exposure to the Other	Lack of awareness of the other	Unaware that the other exists	No feelings for the other	Does not recognize the other
Dualistic Awareness	Awareness of the other	Dualism between good and bad; I am good, the "other" is bad/wrong/unnatural	Is egocentric and/or feels superior to the other; sees self as individual, not connected to anything	Aware that the other exists but does not validate, affirm or become involved with the other
Questioning/ Self-Exploration	Questions perceptions of self and others	Moves away from dualism to relativism	Experiences feelings that make one question own experience	Some conflict or meaningful encounter with the other
Risk-Taking/ Exploration of Otherness	Confronts own perception of the other	Self-reflection paramount	Finds courage to take risk and change behavior toward the other	Confrontation manifests itself in ways external to the individual
Integration/ Validation	Makes complex choices about validating others	Commitment/ interest in self and other	Increased self-confidence	Develops culture of integrity, congruent behaviour, thought, feeling; becomes multicultural (able to interact in and out of own culture); affirms and validates others' experiences

Adapted from Chávez, Guido-DiBrito, and Mallory (2003).

Questioning/Self-Exploration

In this dimension, individuals start to reflect on their values, beliefs, and attitudes. They begin to question, explore and compare these to the beliefs and values of those different from them. Individuals begin to move away from dualistic modes of thinking, and start to see the validity of other perspectives. Initially, this process may be accompanied by fear of losing long-held beliefs, particularly if they are associated with membership in a specific group (for example, a religious group). However, as individuals become more comfortable with broader perspectives, being in this dimension can feel more comfortable and even exciting. Activities that can assist individuals in this dimension are those that encourage self-reflection, involve sharing ideas in small group discussions, and expose individuals to content which incorporates ideas from varied perspectives and within different cultural groups. Educators can introduce varying perspectives through discussion of current topics in the media or through literature and music. Students operating within this dimension can also be encouraged to be more self-reflective through the use of journaling and sharing ideas with others who may have perspectives very different from their own. Cooperative and collaborative group activities can be beneficial in moving students from this dimension to the next.

Risk Taking/Exploration of Otherness

This dimension can be the most uncomfortable for individuals, as it may "pull the rug out" from under long-held values and beliefs. In this dimension, individuals have decided to challenge themselves to understand the worldviews of others, either internally through self-reflection and a search for new ways of thinking, or externally through engaging in situations in which they are compelled to consider alternative viewpoints. An example of this would be immersion in a new culture through travel, or association with groups or individuals whose values and beliefs are vastly different and unfamiliar. Individuals in this dimension can benefit from associating with others engaged in a similar process, so that challenges and dilemmas can be shared. Activities which can encourage individuals in this dimension to continue their process of exploration and risk-taking are: international work or study programs, courses on cultural diversity and other aspects of difference, service learning programs, and involvement in groups concerned with social advocacy and change.

Integration/Validation

Individuals operating within this dimension do not perceive others as having a fixed set of characteristics based on group membership, but as having multiple and complex identities. They are able to find commonalties with others, but also recognize difference without being threatened by it. Individuals operating within the integration/validation dimension are able to interact comfortably with people with different values and beliefs and in a variety of settings and contexts. They have managed to integrate their sense of self with their perception of the other, and continue to strive towards valuing and validating difference wherever they encounter it. This comfort with difference increases over time as they encounter and experience various kinds of difference.

To promote cultural diversity in higher education settings, it is important for faculty, staff, and administrators to value and validate the differences they encounter in the student population. If these differences are not valued, then students from culturally different backgrounds will continue to experience feelings of marginalization, which can negatively affect students' academic performance. Although students who come from groups that are already marginalized in the broader community may be more comfortable with the idea of difference than those from majority cultural groups, this is not always true. Depending on the context and on previous experience, individuals operate in varied dimensions of diversity awareness, which affect how they view difference. The development of diversity awareness is, therefore, relevant to all groups. The Individual Diversity Development Framework can provide a useful starting point for reflection and exploration for professionals in higher education.

Multicultural Education

Multicultural education is a field of study that emerged in the 1960s as a response to issues of social justice and equity in the education system. This approach to teaching and learning was based on principles of cultural pluralism and on elimination of prejudice and discrimination in the educational system. The principle of cultural pluralism asserts the right of different ethnic and cultural groups to retain their language and cultural traditions within a climate of respect for the traditions and values of different groups. This climate can be promoted by providing students with knowledge of the history and backgrounds of different groups, the skills to interact with these groups, and by engendering positive attitudes which counter prejudice and discrimination. Educators can realize these principles by affirming the importance of cultures in the teaching and learning process, and by providing opportunities for equity and academic excellence for all students, regardless of their racial, ethnic, and cultural backgrounds (Bennett, 2001). The goal of equity is not achieved through equality or sameness for all students, but by acknowledging that students come to the learning environment with diverse backgrounds and needs, and that curriculum and teaching practices should respond to this diversity.

The goals of multicultural education focus on change at the individual, classroom, and institutional level, and can be achieved by transforming pedagogical practices, reforming the curriculum, and encouraging multicultural competence (Bennett, 2003). Supportive pedagogy involves instructional strategies, teacher expectations, classroom climates, institutional policies, and practices that enable all students to achieve academic excellence. Curriculum reform can be achieved by including more multicultural and multiethnic knowledge perspectives as well as by changing the Eurocentric content in the curriculum. Multicultural competence prepares students to live in a pluralistic and diverse society, to acknowledge and understand multiple ways of knowing, and to interact and live with people who embrace many different values and traditions.

A Multicultural Education Model

Banks' model of multicultural education provides for implementation of change in response to cultural diversity (Banks, 1997a). Although this model focuses on issues in K-12 education, it can also be applied to higher education settings. This model encompasses five elements: (1) content integration (2) knowledge construction (3) prejudice reduction (4) an equity pedagogy and (5) an empowering learning culture (see Figure 2).

Content Integration

Content integration refers to the need to include information from a variety of cultures into the content of every discipline in order to shift the focus on knowledge perspectives of the dominant group to include those of others. Banks (1997b) offers four approaches to content integration: the contributions, additive, transformative, and social action approach. In the contributions approach, instructors include information about the specific

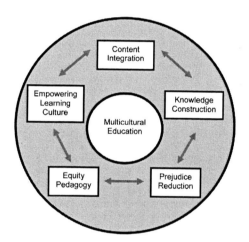

Figure 2: The Elements of Multicultural Education
Adapted from Banks (1997a)

cultural groups. They highlight the aspects of the cultural group evident in readily available resources rather than basing their choices on a deep understanding of what the cultural group considers essential knowledge (Tisdell, 1995).

The additive approach to content integration goes a step further and incorporates additional content that is not represented in the curriculum. However, it is still an add-on to the curriculum rather than a substantial integration of new information. This approach can be incorporated into higher education settings by providing additional course materials or adding to course content. Although it is an improvement over the contributions approach, the additives approach still uses perspectives of the dominant group to determine the added content. The transformative approach to content integration is more radical in that it emerges from different epistemological assumptions. This approach assumes that knowledge construction is not neutral, but is value-laden. Therefore, in order to include knowledge from multiple perspectives, the instructor must make structural changes in the curriculum which foreground alternative and historically marginalized perspectives in all disciplines. Lastly, the social action approach attempts to provide students with the tools to participate in decision making which can lead to social change. While the contributions and additive approaches use essentialist notions of culture to focus on certain visible characteristics of cultural groups and may serve to reinforce stereotypical notions of culture, the last two approaches go further in ensuring that curriculum content addresses issues of multiple centers of knowledge, validating multiple ways of knowing.

The Knowledge Construction Process

The process of knowledge construction is based on the frames of reference, perspectives, and assumptions used when constructing and validating the knowledge produced through each discipline. Some of these perspectives are explicit, but often they are hidden or implicit. In a multicultural classroom, teachers draw attention to these processes of knowledge production so that the perspectives that have influenced the production of certain kinds of knowledge can be revealed and made explicit. Students can thus become aware of the underlying perspectives that inform their assumptions about knowledge within and beyond the classroom. The knowledge construction component of the multicultural model depends on the previous step of content integration in that students have first to be exposed to varying perspectives on the topic covered. The knowledge construction process encourages students to adopt a critical perspective, to ask complex questions about the content they encounter, and to enhance and improve their critical thinking skills and abilities.

Prejudice Reduction

The objective of the prejudice reduction component of the multicultural model is to change or eliminate attitudes and beliefs based on racism, sexism, and other forms of prejudice. Students are encouraged to respect and value difference and to question processes of self-identification that categorize those different from themselves as superior or inferior. Aspects of these efforts to reduce prejudice, based on models of intergroup or intercultural education, have been part of curricula for many years. However, in the multicultural model, the initial goal of intercultural education, promoting harmony between all students by encouraging assimilation into the mainstream culture, has shifted to encouraging students to accept and value diversity. The process of prejudice reduction can be facilitated through the creation of an empowering learning culture, by incorporating curriculum change at different levels, and by examining the knowledge construction process. Teachers can also provide opportunities for students from different backgrounds to work cooperatively and to respect the diverse perspectives within culturally diverse groups.

An Equity Pedagogy

The concept of equity pedagogy is based on the assumption that all students can learn, though they may have diverse ways of learning, influenced by their backgrounds, unique perspectives, and worldviews. To respond to this diversity in the classroom, teachers should provide opportunities for students to learn in different ways from content that is relevant and meaningful to them, and to encourage them to think critically about the perspectives that undergird curriculum content and materials. Equity pedagogy therefore depends on and involves both content integration and knowledge construction. Equity pedagogy relies on teachers' abilities to relate to and understand their students' backgrounds, their learning styles, and the social and cultural influences that have shaped their experiences. However, teachers have to be careful to resist adopting expectations of students based on their membership in specific cultural groups, since these expectations may only serve to reinforce existing stereotypes about students' potential for success.

An Empowering Learning Culture

An empowering learning culture is necessary if students from diverse racial and ethnic groups are to experience equitable and pluralistic learning environments. Changes require concerted effort at all levels of an educational institution. In higher education settings, change should involve faculty, senior administration, centres for teaching and learning, and student bodies (Benick, Newby & Samuel, 1996). The issues that need to be addressed include equitable access, retention, the creation of positive campus climates, adequate support for student learning, and inclusive learning environments.

In Banks' multicultural education model, interrelated parts of the educational system can be shifted or transformed to provide more equitable and pluralistic educational opportunities for all students regardless of their cultural backgrounds. These goals can be achieved by simultaneously working towards the acceptance of diversity at the individual level, and the transformation of pedagogy and curriculum at the classroom and institution level.

Anti-Racist Education

Although the multicultural education movement has made significant contributions to the goal of educational equity, this approach to providing inclusive education for students from diverse backgrounds has been criticized for its association with a celebratory approach to cultural diversity, which focuses on surface aspects of culture such as food, clothing, and entertainment. This decontextualized approach may only provide a superficial understanding of different cultural groups, creating the illusion that these groups are now less unfamiliar and more knowable. Additionally, emphasizing the characteristics of culturally diverse groups can lead to reified and essentialist notions of cultures, ignoring the fact that cultural characteristics are not fixed but fluid and dynamic, and are always mediated by differences within groups such as gender, class, language, religion, as well as varied histories and experiences (Fleras & Elliot, 2003). The movement has also been questioned for insufficient attention to systemic and structural inequities present in the wider society and reproduced in educational institutions (Dei et al., 2000; Marshall, 2002). Multicultural education programs may minimize the inequities faced by marginalized groups or fail to acknowledge that existing inequities are the result of long-standing power imbalances between majority and minority groups, so that groups who do not have access to power and privilege continue to be marginalized.

Critiques of multicultural education have led to deeper examinations of how educational systems can address their shortcomings as well as modified approaches to issues of diversity. One response has been to move from the notion of multicultural education to a model of anti-racist education which highlights and addresses issues of difference, power, and privilege (Dei et al., 2000). Anti-racist educators argue that improved cross-cultural understanding, co-operation, and respect for difference do not address the structural causes of inequity, and that real change can only occur when barriers to inclusive education are challenged at all levels.

An Anti-Racist Education Model

Dei et al. propose a critical integrative approach to inclusive education based on an anti-racist approach. This model "views education as a racially, culturally and politically mediated experience" (Dei et al., 2000, p 8). In contrast to the multicultural model of education, this model emphasizes a more critical approach to diversity by including issues of power, difference and identity. The model encompasses four learning objectives for both the teacher and the student: (1) integrating multiple centres of knowledge (2) recognition and respect for difference (3) effecting social and educational change, equity, access and social justice, and (4) teaching for community empowerment.

Integrating Multiple Centres of Knowledge

This objective involves adding diverse sources of knowledge to the current emphasis on Eurocentric sources so that traditionally marginalized sources can be affirmed and validated. Rather than being an add-on, these centres of knowledge would be integrated into the curriculum at all levels, and would contribute towards the improvement of outcomes for all students, regardless of their cultural background. Integrating multiple centres of knowledge is an objective similar to the content integration element of the multicultural model, but adds the notion of using diverse sources of content to decentre the priority given to traditional sources. The model makes particular reference to three sources of knowledge that have been marginalized. These include indigenous, spiritual, and community knowledge. Indigenous knowledge refers to knowledge that people acquire and use in their everyday lives, based on social and cultural interpretations of their environment. Spiritual knowledge refers to knowledge that is acquired through intuition, revelation or enlightenment, and may or may not be associated with institutionalized religion. Community knowledge is similar to indigenous knowledge and refers to specific content of alternative community-based programs such as cultural and language programs for specific groups. Together, these three types of knowledge provide alternative centres of knowledge which, when integrated into course content, can add to and enrich the learning experiences of all students.

Recognition and Respect for Difference

This objective recognizes the need to consider and value the complex identities of students, and ensure that teaching practices acknowledge and validate these identities. This can be done by designing learning strategies that accommodate diversity of groups, while also recognizing and responding to diversity within groups. Teachers need to recognize and understand their own positions in relation to their students and to work towards uncovering the beliefs, values, and assumptions through which they respond to cultural diversity.

Effecting Social and Educational Change: Equity, Access, and Social Justice

This objective requires that teachers acknowledge the existing inequities in educational structures and environments, understand their role in these structures, and actively advocate for change. Change can occur at all levels of an institution. It can be effected by identifying and challenging existing institutional structures that ignore the needs of minority groups. Policies and programs that address issues of equity can be formulated and implemented to foster a more inclusive climate. The role of the teacher therefore extends from the sphere of the classroom into the community and requires engagement with social and political issues.

Multicultural education, like anti-racist education models, emphasizes the need for understanding difference. It focuses on adding positive images of minority cultural groups into the curriculum, including multiethnic materials, and encouraging harmonious social relations. However, this approach may ignore the influence of existing inequities, asymmetries of power and perceptions of difference that influence social relationships, elements of inequitable access to education that anti-racist education models explicitly address.

Teaching for Community Empowerment

The last objective of the model focuses on building capacity for engagement by working to build and value the social capital and sense of agency of individuals and groups through the active involvement of all concerned groups in educational and institutional decision making. This requires collaboration among teachers, students, administrators, and the community to work for change at a broader level. The multicultural model of education addresses the need for an empowering institutional culture, but does not connect change at the institutional level to change at wider societal levels. The critical integrative model recognizes that changes at the institutional level cannot occur in isolation – they must be considered in light of the existing inequities in society that are reproduced in educational institutions. However, groups have the power and agency to resist and challenge these inequities by actively engaging in and advocating for change.

A critical integrative framework for inclusive education begins with the assertion that the creation of inclusive educational environments requires educators to be aware of how inequities in the classroom are a reflection of inequities in the wider society, to consider the nature of these inequities and the power balances inherent in them, and to employ approaches and strategies which challenge these inequities at all levels to respond to the needs of those who are at the margins.

A Summary of Models

The three models presented in this chapter each address important aspects of teaching and learning in culturally diverse classrooms. They can be used as a starting point for creating inclusive teaching and learning environments at different levels of influence and in different contexts. This process requires change at various levels, beginning with the individual person and learning environment, and moving towards community and societal change. Although the focus of this Guide is to provide strategies for change at the classroom level, it is important to recognize that all levels of change are interconnected. The models presented can be used to derive instructional strategies for the classroom, but also provide a broader context in which change should occur.

The first model presented, the Individual Diversity Development Framework, can be used by educators to understand how their own, as well as students' attitudes towards diversity can be transformed. The model provides suggestions for activities and experiences which would promote and encourage movement along the various dimensions to arrive at a better understanding of the many kinds of difference we encounter in our lives. Although these strategies may be useful in encouraging the diversity development of all students, there may be many kinds of barriers that prevent this development from occurring. These may include the political climate of the campus, fear of reprisal, and deeply embedded values and beliefs about diversity which may take much effort to shift. The models of multicultural and anti-racist education help to shed light on other factors that affect the teaching and learning environment.

The multicultural education model can be used as a guide for creating inclusive teaching and learning environments. Although this model also addresses individual attitudes towards diversity, it provides a more comprehensive way of understanding and implementing change at the classroom level. Banks' (1997a) model of multicultural education can be used to derive appropriate strategies and activities for the culturally diverse classroom by examining how curriculum content and pedagogical practices can be transformed. The model includes five components and each of these can be used to derive specific strategies to create learning environments that respond to diverse needs.

The anti-racist education model responds to critiques of the multicultural education model by including dimensions that address difference from a wider perspective than that of culture, and by acknowledging and addressing issues of systemic and structural inequity which exist in the broader society and are reproduced in educational institutions (Marshall, 2002). It explicitly names the issues of race and sociocultural difference as issues of power and equity rather than as matters of cultural and ethnic variety. Whereas multicultural education focuses on the celebration and understanding of culture, anti-racist education questions how sociocultural differences are used to entrench inequality. The anti-racist education model emphasizes the need for recognizing and respecting diversity at all levels, for transforming curriculum through changes to both content and pedagogy, and for institutional change. This model contends that change at the level of the self, classroom, and institution cannot be sustained unless there are efforts to draw attention to the wider inequities that exist in society. Therefore, both pedagogical and curricular transformation must pay attention to how these inequities may be reproduced in the classroom setting. Progress towards equitable pedagogy involves attending to issues of power, difference, and identity in the classroom, and implementing strategies that are based on careful consideration of these issues.

The main differences between the intercultural, multicultural and ant-racist education models are summarized in Table 2.

Table 2

Intercultural, Multicultural and Anti-Racist Education: Comparisons and Contrasts

	Intercultural Education	Multicultural Education	Anti-Racist Education
Sphere of Activity and Influence	Individual	Individual and class-room	Individual, classroom, educational institutions, and community
Issues	Lack of acceptance and fear of diversity	Eurocentric pedagogy and curriculum content	Inequitable systemic policies and practices
Targeted Change	Individual Attitudes	Individual attitudes, pedagogy and curriculum	Structural change
Long-Term Goals	Acceptance of diversity	Equity in learning environments	Societal equity and justice

This chapter is a revised version of Guo, S., & Jamal, Z. (in press). Nurturing cultural diversity in higher education: A critical review of selected models. *Canadian Journal of Higher Education, 37*(2).

3. The Dynamics of Teaching and Learning

Responding to cultural diversity and maximizing learning for culturally diverse students requires change at many different levels within educational institutions. The models presented in chapter two suggest spheres of influence in which change might occur. The objective of this chapter is to focus on the teaching and learning process in the classroom, and to provide strategies for more culturally responsive teaching and learning environments. This process includes components of teaching and learning which can be used to understand the dynamics of a culturally diverse classroom: students, the instructor, course content, and teaching methods (Marchesani & Adams, 1992).

Students

Selecting appropriate instructional strategies requires instructors to understand the background and experiences of students who are not from the dominant culture. These students may feel marginalized and alienated in classrooms where the strategies and teaching styles are targeted towards students from the dominant cultural groups. For example, practices that focus on competition rather than collaboration, or debate and argument rather than a sharing of perspectives or individual performance may be unfamiliar. The values and beliefs that students from these groups encounter in the classroom may be quite different from their own, and instructors need to have some understanding of these differences in order to select the most appropriate methods of instruction.

Students from different cultural groups may also have different conceptions of what is worth knowing. If the curriculum and instructional strategies are made up of materials based primarily on a Eurocentric perspective, students may feel that their learning styles, beliefs, values, and experiences are of less importance, thus increasing feelings of being an 'outsider'. The importance of considering, understanding, and validating student differences is emphasized in all three models presented in the previous chapter – the intercultural framework, the multicultural model and the anti-racist model.

Instructor

The second component in the dynamics of teaching and learning is the role and behaviour of the instructor. Personal values, beliefs, and attitudes towards diversity influence how instructors communicate and interact with their students. Instructors may have the tendency to assume that their values and beliefs are widely held and valued. Instructors should make the effort to examine their own values and beliefs, and to explore how these have been influenced by their social and cultural backgrounds as well as their prior experiences with diversity. The Framework of Individual Diversity Development (see Table 1) can assist instructors in assessing their own attitudes and beliefs towards the diversity they encounter in the classroom and to behave in ways that are inclusive rather than exclusive.

Course Content

Both multicultural and anti-racist models of education emphasize the importance of creating a pluralistic curriculum that incorporates diverse social and cultural perspectives. This includes an examination of the course content, the texts and materials used, and the perspectives validated within those texts. Curriculum can be changed at different levels, ranging from a simple addition of materials on specific cultural groups, to a more transformative approach where knowledge and texts from different perspectives and traditions are integrated into curricula design. A transformed curriculum "encourages new ways of thinking and incorporates new methodologies, so that different epistemological questions are raised, old assumptions are questioned, subjective data sources are considered, and prior theories are either revised or invalidated" (Marchesani & Adams, 1992, p.15-16).

Teaching Methods

The fourth component of this framework addresses the teaching methods used in the classroom. Instructional strategies can have a major impact on the interactions that occur between teachers and students, and among students. This component suggests that changes to instructional strategies can play a major role in transforming classrooms into sites that both respect diversity and promote student learning. The use of a wider range of instructional strategies can help to respond to diverse learning styles, perspectives, and cultural values, and promote learning for both dominant and minority cultural and linguistic groups. This can lead to social action where students use new cognitive lenses to push for social change.

4. Culturally Inclusive Teaching Strategies

The experiences that students have in the classroom have a significant impact on their cognitive and affective development, their acquisition of knowledge, educational goals, interpersonal skills, and level of effort (Cabrera et al., 2002). Students' experiences can be deliberately enhanced by building inclusive classroom environments where instructors use a wide variety of instructional strategies and pay close attention to the impact of these strategies on student motivation, levels of participation, and outcomes. We have categorized strategies for creating inclusive and effective teaching environments into five broad areas: (1) creating a positive classroom environment (2) diversifying curriculum content (3) instructional strategies and activities for learning (4) assessment strategies and (5) role of instructors.

Creating a Positive Classroom Environment

The first step in addressing the needs of culturally diverse students is to create a positive classroom environment that recognizes, respects, and validates difference and diversity. Naeth (1993) suggests that in a positive classroom environment "students should feel respected, accepted and valued" (p. 8). This includes creating space for students to express diverse opinions, beliefs, and perspectives in an environment that encourages dialogue and discussion without the fear of bias and prejudice. A large part of a positive environment is dependent on the interaction that occurs in the classroom between the instructor and students, as well as between students. If interaction follows the normal patterns that exist outside the classroom in the wider context, then any structures of inequity that exist externally may potentially be reproduced in the classroom. To create a positive social climate, instructors should pay close attention to the patterns of interaction in the classroom, since these climates do not generally occur without the use of specific and deliberate strategies. For example, educators might deliberately use strategies that resist these patterns, and instead create a climate that is safe and productive. A safe classroom environment also contributes to student learning since "people who feel unsafe, unconnected, and disrespected are unlikely to be motivated to learn" (Wlodkowski & Ginsberg, 1995, p. 2).

The models of multicultural and anti-racist education presented earlier in this Guide both address the issue of creating positive climates in the classroom. Both the element of prejudice reduction in the multicultural education model and the objective of recognition and respect for difference in the anti-racist education model emphasize the importance of promoting attitudes and beliefs in which diversity and difference are respected and valued. Although a key goal of higher education is to create and transmit a body of knowledge, students from a variety of cultural groups also bring to this environment many different experiences that can provide new insights, which add to, enhance, and question this knowledge. A climate of inclusiveness will help to acknowledge and validate diverse traditions and experiences, and can contribute to the learning of all students.

The following strategies can be used to create a supportive classroom environment for students from culturally diverse backgrounds (Naeth, 1993; Kees, 2003; Jones, 2004).

Get to Know Your Students Individually as Much as Possible

- Learn students' names as soon as possible by using name cards, name tags or other reminders. Make special efforts to learn the pronunciation and spelling of all names.

- Arrive early in the classroom and use this opportunity to talk individually with students who are also early. Stay later to connect with those who stay behind. Use opportunities such as office visits by students to get to know student backgrounds and areas of interest.

- Maintain contact with students, request feedback from them, and pay attention to students' individual experiences, especially those which may shape the ways that they participate in the learning process.

- Allow students the opportunity to share their personal history, including their backgrounds, their educational histories and goals, and their motivation for participating in the course or program. This helps to validate the unique experiences and contributions of each person in the classroom.

- Remember and acknowledge personal information they share in class.

- Use email to communicate with students to increase opportunities for contact, to maintain contact on an ongoing basis, and to respond to questions and issues on a more timely basis than may be otherwise possible.

Create a Physically Welcoming Environment

- Whenever possible, arrange the physical seating in the room so that the instructor and the students can all make eye contact with each other. In a U-shaped seating arrangement, vary the position of the instructor so that the instructor is not at the head of the U-shape all the time.

- Periodically arrange the room so that students can be seated in face-to-face groups to support group activities.

Create a Positive Emotional Climate

- Use icebreaker activities to encourage students to get to know each other. Encourage students to learn each other's names to create a sense of rapport in the classroom. Avoid assigning English names to non-English students. Call students by the names that they give you.

- Communicate at the outset that student participation in the class will be encouraged and welcomed. Identify that participation can include active listening as well as speaking.

- Model acceptance and respect for diverse views and opinions.

- Encourage questions and participation in discussions. Meanwhile, respect learners who prefer active listening.

- Establish clear ground rules at the beginning of the class about communication norms, including how inappropriate statements (such as racist or sexist comments) will be dealt with.

- Ask for student feedback on how they feel about the classroom climate. Ensure that there is opportunity for anonymous as well as public feedback.

- Encourage students to exchange email addresses to foster interaction among students.

Create an Inclusive Environment

- Use inclusive language in the classroom to help create a positive classroom climate. For example, attempt to use appropriate words to describe ethnic, cultural, or other groups, according to the groups' preferences.

- Treat all students equally by valuing the ideas and opinions of all students.

- Intervene if any student demonstrates behaviour that is disrespectful to other students.

- Include and respond to all students equally in discussions and activities.

- Avoid interacting with students in ways that may be uncomfortable for them.

- To reduce their sense of anxiety and increase their sense of safety, avoid repeatedly calling on individual students.

- Without focusing on specific students, invite class members who are comfortable doing so to share examples from their own backgrounds.

Diversifying Curriculum Content

Use of the Multicultural and Anti-Racist Education Models to Diversify Curriculum Content

Chapter two presented models for nurturing cultural diversity and described two that are relevant to the task of diversifying curriculum content. Both the multicultural and anti-racist education models highlight the importance of changes to curriculum content to make learning environments more inclusive of students from culturally and linguistically diverse backgrounds. Modifying course content is an evolving and dynamic process, rather than one in which the outcome can be pre-determined (Kitano, 1997b). It requires continual and ongoing effort to strive towards a particular set of goals, to judge the effectiveness of the results, and to adjust the approaches and modify strategies along the way. Each instructor chooses approaches and strategies according to the nature of the course and its particular goals. The following section provides a number of strategies useful in moving towards more pluralistic course content.

General Strategies for Diversifying Curriculum Content

Highlight Different Ways of Knowing

- The various disciplines within the academic community consider different ways of knowing most valid, and tend to privilege those approaches. Highlight the validity of different ways of knowing and provide examples of the consequences of adopting a specific approach while ignoring others (Dei et al., 2000).

Include the Lives, Experiences, Histories, and Contributions of Major Figures from Various Traditions and Groups

- Add the histories of prominent figures from culturally and linguistically diverse groups when discussing contributions to a given discipline.

- Include new research and scholarship from groups that have traditionally been underrepresented or ignored.

Use the Appropriate Terms to Refer to Various Groups

- Use inclusive and appropriate language to refer to cultural and ethnic groups, based on the groups' preferences. Point out the use of inappropriate language in texts and course materials and use them as an example of how language has historically reflected the way in which difference is regarded, and contributes to how we construct and view difference (Dei et al., 2000).

Present Alternative Perspectives on Key Concepts and Ideas

- Provide reading material that presents a concept or idea from different theoretical perspectives. Emphasize the multiplicity of views and perspectives. For example, in a course on leadership, in addition to Western-based models of leadership, draw upon theories of leadership from other traditions (Kitano, 1997b). This would broaden the discussion of leadership to include new ways of looking at this topic.

- Invite guest speakers with various perspectives and opinions to enrich course content and enhance the perspectives presented in the course.

- Arrange course content so that different perspectives on an issue can be examined and compared.

- Select course materials authored by writers from minority groups.

- Use *compare and contrast* questions in quizzes and tests to highlight different ideas and opinions.

- Encourage students to consider opposing or different viewpoints, and to express their opinions about these. Ensure that the classroom climate is one that provides a sense of safety to accommodate this process.

- When responding to comments, distinguish between facts and opinions. Incorrect facts can be corrected, but individual opinions based on differences in perspectives can be acknowledged as valid, even if there is disagreement.

- Challenge students to think through their comments by offering other perspectives during class discussions.

- Use a *one-minute paper* assignment at the end of class. Ask students to respond anonymously in writing to ideas or statements they would challenge or have different opinions about.

- Have students work in groups to defend a certain position on a topic. Have groups share their various positions, emphasizing that the objective is not to decide on a superior or best position, but to develop multiple perspectives.

- Avoid the use of texts and materials that use negative stereotypes. If these cannot be avoided, identify the stereotypes and present alternative perspectives.

Highlight Processes of Knowledge Construction and Validation

The purpose of these strategies is to highlight the process of knowledge construction and encourage critical thinking about the perspectives from which course content is presented. What counts as legitimate knowledge? How and why does knowledge get constructed the way it does? Whose knowledge is considered valuable? Whose knowledge is silenced? Is knowledge racialized?

- When discussing a text or journal article, ask students to consider the perspective presented in the material. Who are the authors of the text and what perspective do they present? Are there biases in the way the materials are presented? Are the perspectives of minority groups represented? Is the information presented in a way that implies that this is the only perspective that is valid?

- Analyze how the media and curriculum materials portray people from diverse backgrounds and cultural groups. Who is producing these images and what is their purpose? What is your reaction to them? Is your reaction to these images shared by most people, and why? Are there other ways to interpret these images?

- Emphasize the importance of seeing different perspectives and of understanding the context in which these perspectives have been developed. This includes an examination of how social and cultural context has an impact on how people adopt certain ideas and beliefs, and how these ideas gain validity.

Increase Students' Awareness of Diversity Issues

- Encourage student participation in extra curricular events that promote awareness of diversity issues (international week, special events that mark achievements of people from minority or unrecognized groups, extra-curricular lectures and seminars that address issues of diversity, community forums on diversity and inclusion, etc.).

- Encourage students to get involved with various groups on campus and in the community that advocate for the rights of minority groups. Provide information on these groups and events they organize.

Instructional Strategies and Activities for Learning

Diversifying the curriculum is only one element required to create inclusive classrooms: appropriate pedagogical understandings and practices also support this goal. Instructors need to understand their own values and beliefs about difference and diversity, the kinds of differences that students bring to the classroom environment, and the most appropriate practices to respond to these differences. The three models presented in chapter two of the Guide can assist in this process of change.

To respond to these cultural, epistemological and value-based differences, instructors can incorporate diverse teaching strategies and methods in order to reach as many students as possible. Equity pedagogy and respect for difference do not require instructors to identify specific groups of students on the basis of their supposed particular learning styles, since students from culturally diverse backgrounds as well as students from majority cultural groups all exhibit much diversity amongst themselves. The instructor should therefore get to know the students in a specific course as much as possible, and deliberately vary the instructional strategies and activities to accommodate diversity. Inclusive environments can be created by "incorporating teaching strategies and learning activities that capitalize on students' experiences and learning strengths; include opportunities for personal participation and growth; and foster skills important to informed citizenship, such as critical thinking, decision making, social participation, and intergroup interaction" (Kitano, 1997b, p. 26).

This section suggests a number of instructional strategies to facilitate learning in culturally diverse classrooms. These strategies have been organized into four broad categories: (1) encouraging interaction and participation (2) incorporating collaborative learning strategies (3) addressing diverse learning styles and (4) contextualizing teaching and the curriculum.

Encouraging Interaction and Participation

Students engage in classroom discussions and other group activities with varying levels of comfort. The following strategies may be used to promote equitable participation and interaction in the classroom.

- Build a strong sense of rapport and community within the classroom and focus on this objective at the beginning of the course. The strategies presented in the section on icebreaker and warm up activities can be used for this.

- Use verbal and non-verbal messages to reward student participation. Listen attentively and equally to all students. Make eye contact and use students' names as often as possible when responding to questions or comments. Meanwhile, be aware that in some cultures direct eye contact with the teacher may be viewed as a sign of disrespect.

- Pay particular attention to the levels of student participation in the first few classes, since these will set the tone for future classes. Ensure that all students have had a chance to participate in the first few weeks.

- Attend to the kind of strategies and activities that promote participation and those that seem to hinder it, and adjust strategies accordingly. Ask students for feedback about the activities and strategies that motivate them to participate.

- If a few people dominate large group discussions, introduce small group discussion to allow the marginalized or intimidated student more opportunity to contribute to the discussion.

- Vary the kinds of questions you ask: include questions that require recall of information, open-ended questions that require divergent thinking, as well as others that require providing examples or personal experiences relevant to the topic under discussion. Different students may respond to different kinds of questions: providing opportunities for a variety of responses helps to increase the number of students who respond.

- Ask for clarification of questions and comments when necessary rather than making assumptions about what students mean.

- In order to provide more equitable opportunities for participation increase wait time, especially for those questions that involve difficult or complex subject matter (Sadker & Sadker, 1992). Wait time is the amount of time that instructors stay silent after asking questions in the classroom. When wait time is very short, students who are most comfortable answering questions and participating in classroom discussions will be more likely to respond, providing little opportunity for those students who may not be as comfortable participating, or for whom English is an additional language. Waiting slightly longer for an answer indicates to students that their participation is valued and allows them time to understand the question and formulate a reply. Wait at least 10 seconds to allow for student reflection.

- To promote interaction among students, encourage students to respond to each other's questions and comments. For example, you can ask the class, "Does anyone have a response or thought about this comment?" Avoid prolonged conversation with one or more vocal students.

- Communicate that students' contributions are valued by highlighting how their comments contribute to the discussion, by asking other students to build on the ideas contributed, by requesting elaboration or explanation of the thought process behind an idea, and by summarizing the different views or comments provided.

- Be positive when responding to questions and comments, since negative remarks will deter other students from participating, especially those who are already tentative or uncertain about how their contributions will be received.

- Ask students to facilitate discussions and generate questions on particular topics or assigned readings, either individually or in pairs.

- Assign students roles such as timekeeper, summarizer or recorder during small or large group discussions, especially students who have participated less than others and who may be more comfortable in roles with clearly defined ways of interacting.

- Encourage students to share resources related to course content, and to start or continue discussions on topics relevant to course content.

- Where available, use technology such as a learning management system to create an online learning community. This may provide an opportunity for students who are not comfortable speaking in class an alternative way of interacting with each other.

Incorporating Collaborative Learning Strategies

Collaborative and cooperative learning strategies require students to work together in small groups with the goal of maximizing each student's participation and learning. These strategies encourage higher levels of communication, interaction, dialogue, and shared learning than does the traditional lecture format. The teacher's role is extended from providing information through lectures to the facilitation and coordination of student groups. Collaborative learning strategies help students develop higher level reasoning and thinking skills (Panitz & Panitz, 1998). For collaborative learning to occur, students should be interdependent, should be accountable to the group for their portion of the work, should use appropriate communication and interpersonal skills, and should be able to reflect on the effectiveness of their group's joint learning and consider ways to improve it (Venable, 2004).

Although the benefits of collaborative learning apply to all students, this group of strategies can be especially helpful to students from culturally diverse backgrounds. Diversity in cultural backgrounds could be reflected in differences in learning and communication styles that may be better accommodated in small learning groups rather than in large class discussions. For example, students from cultures that value individualism are accustomed to communication styles where challenge and debate is encouraged, whereas students from cultures that value the collective expect and may prefer styles that encourage cooperation and collaboration (Wang & Folger, 2004). Working in small groups can encourage normally quiet students who may be reluctant to participate in large group discussions, particularly those whose first language is not English, to voice their opinions and thoughts. Collaborative learning strategies can provide group support for students, increase opportunity for interaction and discussion, and contribute towards a positive classroom environment. Such an environment encourages cooperation rather than competition, develops learning communities, and encourages understanding among diverse groups of students as well as between students and instructors. Collaborative learning emphasizes the process of learning rather than the end product. Learning processes depend on the prior experiences of students, their skill levels, and the knowledge base they bring to the classroom. By focusing on process, collaborative learning provides opportunities to reveal, value, and accommodate this diversity.

The benefits of collaborative learning have been documented by a number of studies (Panitz & Panitz, 1998). In one study investigating the effectiveness of collaborative learning, the authors found that students from minority groups preferred collaborative learning to other learning methods and that it influenced the level of openness to diversity by changing negative attitudes towards students from different backgrounds (Cabrera et al., 2002). Collaborative learning also had a positive impact on student outcomes, promoted interpersonal and group communication skills, and generally encouraged more active participation in the learning process.

Collaborative learning can also be promoted through the use of educational technology tools such as learning management systems. These tools can be used informally; students can post questions and comments about course content or assignments and receive responses from either the instructor or other students. Alternatively, the tools can be used for more structured work. These can include online study groups, group projects and assignments, and other collaborative strategies. The instructor can make participation in these online activities optional or a required element of the course. Online collaboration can increase class participation and communication and create an environment of dialogue, interchange, and problem solving, fostering critical thinking (Bullen, 1997; Guo, 2000, 2005). It can also provide opportunities for students to discuss issues without the limitations of place and time. It offers students more time to think over their responses, and eliminates wait time when asking questions or providing answers (Dewiyanti, Brand-Gruwel, & Jochems, 2005). Students who are not comfortable speaking in class or who are from different linguistic backgrounds may be more inclined to participate online (Bates & Poole, 2003). However, before using technology for teaching and learning, the instructor should ensure that all students have access to the required technology, and the skills required to use the technology.

Types of Cooperative Groups

Venable (2004) identifies three types of cooperative groups typical of collaborative learning: formal groups, informal groups, and long-term groups. These types of groups can be used exclusively or can be combined in order to achieve specific goals. Formal collaborative groups are structured to accomplish specific objectives. The group is assigned a fixed task and stays together until the task is complete. The task requires students to meet on a regular basis. The formal group may also be a study group in which students meet periodically to review and clarify course material. In contrast, informal cooperative groups are formed for the duration of a class, or part of it. Members may rotate through groups to accomplish short tasks such as discussing an assigned reading, completing a class activity, or summarizing and presenting a short topic. Long-term groups are formed for the purpose of accomplishing goals such as a term project involving a considerable amount of research. These groups require more intragroup maintenance and attention to group process.

Promoting Diversity Awareness Through Group Work

If possible, form groups that are demographically heterogeneous without completely isolating individuals from their natural support structures. Practically, this means that where any student categories appear in small numbers, avoid always distributing them "one to a group." After the assigned task has been completed, ask the groups to consider the process that was used. Were differing opinions expressed? How did the group deal with these? Were there major similarities and differences between perspectives? Did these differences cause rethinking on any issues? These reflective activities encourage students to examine how they respond to diversity, and the differences as well as commonalties that can exist in diverse groups. The Individual Diversity Development Framework, presented in the section on models for nurturing diversity (see chapter two), may be a good resource for students to use when considering their experiences in diverse groups.

Icebreaker and Warm-up Activities

Introducing collaborative learning strategies at the beginning of the course allows students the opportunity to get to know one another; this can be accomplished with various icebreaker and warm-up activities (Panitz & Panitz, 1998). The early use of collaborative activities can help students feel connected to others in the classroom and thus establish a positive classroom climate in which collaborative activities can evolve.

- Include activities that build a sense of team identity, such as choosing a team name, creating a team symbol or mascot, and introducing a team vision. Promote interdependence and teamwork by encouraging students to exchange contact information for the purpose of setting up informal groups for study and review, discussing the characteristics of effective teams, setting ground rules for team process, and identifying strategies for dealing with team members who ignore these rules (Cuseo, n.d.).

- Ask pairs of students to share their academic history as well as their extra curricular interests. Use this activity to encourage student questions about the course. Record the questions on a flip chart to post on the wall. After initial introductions, use the items on the flip chart to start a class discussion.

- A card-sort activity allows students to walk around the classroom and meet other students. Provide each student with an index card illustrating an item in a specific category (e.g. food, living thing, item of clothing, month of birth, etc.). Ask students to circulate and to find other students whose card illustrates the same category. Students who have found all others in the same category identify themselves as a team. This exercise can be used as an icebreaker or to form teams for a subsequent cooperative activity.

The Carousel

The purpose of this collaborative learning activity is to encourage high levels of group interaction and dialogue and to encourage students to contribute their knowledge and perspective in a collaborative group process (Jones, 2004). It can be used to review students' current knowledge of a topic before the unit starts, or as a review to summarize student knowledge of the particular topic. The instructor posts a number of open-ended questions about a particular topic on large sheets of paper posted on the wall. In groups of four or five, students select one chart and answer questions posted on it. They then move to the next chart and build on the previous group's work, validating their responses with check marks and adding new responses. Each group uses a different coloured marker to distinguish one group's responses from another's. As the groups rotate through the charts, they have to think more critically and dig more deeply into their knowledge base to come up with additional responses to the questions.

Jigsaw Activity

In the jigsaw activity, first developed in the early 1970s by Elliot Aronson and his students at the University of Texas and the University of California, teams of students are assigned a topic, and each member of the team becomes an expert on some aspect of the topic. All the experts in a subtopic gather together in a new team to review the material in the subtopic and then go back to their original teams to teach others and to reflect on the process. Each subtopic is a piece of the jigsaw, and combined with the other subtopics, provides the team with an understanding of a bigger picture of the larger topic. A variation is to give each team a quiz on the material, encouraging interdependence in the learning process.

Addressing Diverse Learning Styles

Learning styles are the preferred methods through which students perceive, assimilate, organize, and apply information. Personal characteristics such as age, gender, interests, goals, and motivation levels can affect learning styles, as well as social and cultural influences. The literature on learning styles describes the many different dimensions along which learning styles can vary and provides inventories and assessment tools that can be used to determine students' predominant learning styles. Introducing the recommended instructional strategies appropriate to different learning styles found in this literature can contribute to creating effective learning environments. Although there is general agreement that some congruence or match between teaching and learning styles leads to more effective engagement and enhances learning, there is also some evidence to suggest the value of a mismatch to promote deeper learning and new ways of thinking and learning (Coffield, Moseley, Hall & Kathryn, 2004).

Interest in how learning styles differ among students has extended to a discussion of the relationship between cultural background and learning styles (Ladson-Billings, 1992). Although it may be useful for instructors to know how specific cultural groups tend to vary in their learning styles, individuals within a specific cultural group may exhibit as many or more different learning styles among themselves as are found when comparing different groups. In a culturally diverse classroom, culture-specific information may be of limited value. The most useful approach to dealing with a variety of learning styles is for instructors to become familiar with the literature on learning styles and to use a range of instructional strategies to address diverse learning styles (Anderson & Adams, 1992).

Some general strategies that may be used to address diverse learning styles and to individualize learning:

- Incorporate a variety of visual elements in the delivery of course content such as simple sketches, diagrams, photos, images, and graphs.

- Make connections between the course material being presented, the material that has been previously presented and other areas of knowledge that students may have.

- Provide a variety of materials that emphasize conceptual understanding and apply those materials to solving discipline-specific problems.

- Provide students with opportunities to practice the concepts taught where applicable.

- Incorporate the use of technology in instructional strategies where possible. This could range from the use of learning management systems for a variety of activities to the simple use of an internet connection in the classroom to incorporate online resources.

- Provide time for reflection during the class so that students can think about the course content presented. This time could be used for writing, journaling, or group reflection.

- Vary the activities in the class between lectures, large group discussions, and small group activities.

- Use a variety of assessment strategies.

- Ask for student feedback about the degree to which the instruction is useful and responsive to diverse needs.

Contextualizing Teaching and the Curriculum

Teachers should probe and reflect on the existing knowledge and cultural experiences of their students and use those insights to enrich and contextualize learning experiences.

Allow Students Opportunities for Choice and Decision Making

- Present the course outline and ask students to identify areas they would like to add or emphasize during the course.

- To accommodate diverse needs and learning styles, offer students more choice in the kinds of assignments that are required and in the way the assignments are to be completed.

- Encourage students to choose their own topics for class essays and other assignments to increase the sense of personal relevance and motivation.

- Provide suggestions for optional reading on topics in areas that individual students may wish to explore in more depth.

Provide Context for Abstract Ideas and Concepts

Students are more likely to retain meaningful, relevant information than abstract facts. Contextual teaching provides examples and analogies that are meaningful to students. It encourages students to draw on relevant knowledge acquired from their specific linguistic and cultural backgrounds. Simulations, role-plays, case studies, and problem solving activities can also help to connect abstract concepts to students' experiences (Kitano, 1997b).

- Simulations and role-playing activities can be useful when students are required to practice their skills and knowledge within a certain context. They foster creativity, allow diverse responses to the same problem, and help link concepts to personal experiences. These can be especially effective in disciplines such as nursing and social work, where students are required to apply what they have learned to real situations but can explore different ways of applying their knowledge. Participation in role-play activities should initially be voluntary to reduce anxiety in students who are unwilling to demonstrate their skills in front of a group.

- Case studies provide another way of contextualizing concepts and ideas so that they seem less abstract. In case studies, students analyze either real or simulated scenarios and provide their own unique solutions to particular problems. Like simulation and role-playing activities, this method allows students to contribute to solutions to a problem from their own unique perspectives. Case studies also provide greater opportunity for participation and collaboration among students.

Assessment Strategies

Two kinds of changes to assessment practices can support inclusive teaching. The first is to modify traditional assessment practices to make them more appropriate for diverse students, and the second is to introduce alternative forms of assessment.

Modifying Traditional Assessment Strategies

The following are some recommendations for modifying traditional assessment practices:

- Ensure that students have the required knowledge and skills to participate in the assessment activity. Instructors should clarify the skills required for both course and assessment participation so that students can take steps to remedy the gaps wherever possible. It may be useful for instructors to refer students to campus resources and support services that can provide assistance such as tutoring, language skill development, strategies for note-taking and exam writing, research skills, time management, and study skills.

- Provide clear instructions and prepare students for all assignments ahead of time. For tests, quizzes, and exams, inform students of the format of the test, the course content to be covered, grading procedures, and helpful strategies for studying and writing the tests. The norms of writing tests and exams may be obvious and familiar to some students who are used to this form of assessment but may be unfamiliar to others. Clear instructions will provide valuable information and help to reduce anxiety. In addition, students may find it useful to have access to some good models of writing against which to judge their work.

- Communicate the expectations of the assessment strategy as related to the objectives. Students who speak English as an additional language may have trouble following instructions for an assignment if the language is dense and the instructions are not clearly worded. For essay assignments, describe the length, the writing style required, and the content expected.

- Help students to break down major assignments into smaller steps. Instructors can also structure assignments so that students can submit each piece separately, enabling the students to improve the quality of the final assignment.

- Encourage students to collaborate and consult each other on their work, even for individual assignments such as essays. Students can form small groups to discuss their topics and to edit and comment on each other's work. Encourage and provide support for the creation of study and support groups.

- If the assessment strategy includes assigning marks for class participation, acknowledge a variety of ways in which participation can occur. Examples may include contributing a journal or newspaper article for class discussion, providing additional resources that are relevant to class content, listening carefully and providing encouragement to others, engaging in discussion with one or two other students rather than the whole class, and providing written responses to questions (Fenwick & Parsons, 2000).

- Ask for input on assessment criteria. This can include developing criteria with the students by providing them anonymous samples that you have clearly identified as good, acceptable, and poor. Then have groups of students flesh out the assessment criteria for each sample. Conduct a discussion in the class using this input and collectively develop criteria for assessment.

Alternative Assessment Strategies

Alternative assessment strategies can provide a more holistic approach to assessment and can help to address diverse learning styles and experiences. Offer students some choice of assessment strategies to validate their preferences and to assist them in taking more responsibility for their own learning.

Alternatives to Written Assignments

To accommodate diverse learning styles, allow students to present the results of their work in forms other than the traditional written assignments, including:

- reading logs

- insight cards outlining student responses to an assigned reading

- oral reports

- panel presentations

- group projects

- vignettes, small productions, or demonstrations

- concept maps, slide presentations, collages or exhibits.

Two specific examples of alternative assessment practices are portfolio assessment and dynamic assessment.

Portfolio Assessment

A portfolio is a collection of work completed by students over a period of time. Portfolios may include papers and articles written by the students, the results of assessments, tests, exams or inventories, samples of artwork, and journal entries (Fenwick & Parsons, 2000). Using portfolios for student assessment offers students a greater degree of flexibility in the assessment process. Rather than measuring growth against a set external standard, portfolios can be a way to judge the learning that has occurred over time, documenting the student's activities and progress. Student portfolios are useful for assessing non-cognitive development and can provide extended feedback on growth over time (Jalomo Jr., 2000). Portfolio assessments are particularly useful for students returning to the classroom as adults and for documenting field and work experience. Portfolio assessments can either replace more traditional forms of assessment or can be added as a further means of measuring learning. They encourage collaboration between students and instructors since they require ongoing consultation and mentoring.

Dynamic Assessment

Conventional assessment methods assume that the evaluator is an objective observer with the ability to make judgments about the person being evaluated. This notion of objectivity does not take into account the varied social, cultural, and linguistic backgrounds of some students, thereby placing them at a disadvantage when applying traditional assessment measures (Fenwick & Parsons, 2000). Dynamic assessment is based on the idea that learning is an ongoing process rather than a discrete activity with a fixed start and ending point. This method of assessment focuses on the learner's growth and development, and considers the impact of contextual factors such as the abilities and learning styles of the learner, the learner's perspectives, language differences, and links to community. It also values the learner's previous knowledge, skills, and perception of self.

Dynamic assessment may be implemented in many different ways. Reflective writing and story telling, for example, can document the learner's progress. Journals provide a tool for reflection and for documenting progress and growth. Students may describe critical incidents which have been triggers for learning, or create a visual representation symbolizing the learning that has occurred. Dynamic assessment may also include the application of learning to real-life problems and situations.

Role of Instructors

The role of instructors in creating inclusive learning environments includes attention and thoughtfulness about personal values and beliefs about diversity, developing competency in the use of varied instructional strategies, and modification of curriculum content. Chesler (2002) provides a number of suggestions for faculty who are working towards creating more inclusive classrooms.

- Evaluate your teaching methods by asking for responses from students about their level of comfort in the classroom, and the effectiveness of the learning strategies being used. Ask for feedback about the level of inclusiveness they perceive in the classroom.

- Develop your own strategies that are most suitable for your context.

- Invite a colleague to observe a teaching situation and to provide a critical view of whether your classroom is culturally responsive and is meeting the needs of all students. If there is room for improvement, elicit ideas about possible strategies for creating a more inclusive environment.

- Become more aware of the culture and histories of groups that your students identify with and encourage students to relate concepts to their own experiences.

- Seek out resources that can assist in the task of modifying content and diversifying instructional strategies. These can include conferences, seminars, and university centres that provide professional development in teaching practices, and online resources. Create a network with other instructors committed to the same goals, and exchange information about new resources and ideas as they become available.

- Advocate for and contribute to efforts to create more equitable educational organizations so that efforts to create change at the classroom level are supported and accompanied by broader structural and systemic changes.

5. Strategies for Linguistically Diverse Students

The aim of this chapter is to provide strategies that are more inclusive of students whose first language is not English. It describes how instructors can be more inclusive of this group of students, create a welcoming environment for them, facilitate the learning of course content, and assist in the development of their English language skills.

Assessing Needs

The first step in determining the needs of linguistically diverse students is to gain knowledge of their backgrounds and previous educational experiences to determine their needs in the classroom (Kinsella, 1997). This information can be gathered through brief questionnaires, journal entries, or student profile forms. The only commonality among these diverse students may be that English is an additional language for them. They may be international students pursuing degrees, exchange students planning to return to their countries after one or two semesters, recent immigrants or refugees planning permanent residency in Canada, or students who have studied in francophone school environments. The background information gathered can then be used to modify existing strategies or to add new strategies to accommodate student needs. The instructor may also refer students to support systems on campus to ease the transition into a linguistically unfamiliar environment.

Language Proficiency

Cummins (as cited in Kinsella, 1997) provides a theoretical basis for the linguistic challenges faced by non-native speakers of English. Cummins distinguishes between two types of proficiency in language: basic interpersonal communication skills (BICS) and cognitive-academic language proficiency (CALP). BICS is the contextualized language of everyday conversations and is acquired through interactions at school, work, and in social contexts. In contrast, CALP is the decontextualized academic language that is required to perform successfully in academic environments. If students demonstrate English conversational skills, the instructor cannot assume that students also have CALP. Cummins found that competence in CALP can take several years longer than in BICS. Cummins argues that BICS and CALP operate along two intersecting continua. The first continuum distinguishes between context-embedded situations and context-reduced situations. Context-embedded situations provide clues to assist in the use of language, as in social and work situations which involve conversation about everyday topics. In contrast, context-reduced situations such as academic environments provide fewer clues to the student.

The second continuum addresses the level of cognitive demand placed on the learner. These two continua provide four quadrants in which students operate. Most academic environments are cognitively demanding and context-reduced, implying that they require a greater level of language proficiency. Awareness of these two continua can assist instructors to anticipate the needs of linguistically diverse students, and to select strategies to support students' learning, and to recognize areas of potential challenge both in classroom situations and in assigned coursework.

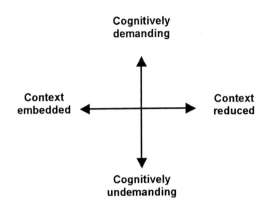

Figure 3: Factors Influencing Language Proficiency

Strategies for the Classroom

Linguistically diverse students face several challenges in academic settings. Assimilating information from extended lectures may pose a problem, since this requires extensive processing of information and perhaps simultaneous translation into their dominant language. Linguistically diverse students may be reluctant to participate in class discussion, even if they have significant contributions to make, for a variety of reasons. They may feel that they do not comprehend the material adequately. They may be unfamiliar with specialized terminology and its pronunciation in English, or unsure of the unspoken rules for interaction in the classroom. Students may not have the listening and study skills that are essential in college classrooms. Instructors often assume that these skills are a prerequisite and do not deliberately include the teaching of these skills with course content. To address these challenges Kinsella (1997) suggests a range of strategies that can be used to create inclusive learning environments for linguistically diverse students. These strategies fall into three broad areas: (1) providing increased contextual information and linguistic support (2) providing specific learning and study approaches and (3) providing greater opportunities for classroom interaction and participation.

Providing Increased Contextual Information and Linguistic Support

- Speak clearly and at a normal speech rate, emphasize key ideas and words, and provide enough pauses to allow time for questions and note-taking. Avoid the use of long-winded or convoluted sentences. Some students may also have trouble with idioms and culturally based examples, and these should be used sparingly or clarified.

- Double or triple your usual wait time in a linguistically diverse classroom as students who speak English as an additional language have to mentally translate discussion into their dominant language and then translate their responses back into English.

- Ask for clarification when student responses are not clear rather than making assumptions about what a student may be trying to communicate.

- Use visuals such as diagrams, charts, pictures, and overheads to aid comprehension.

- Ensure that notes written on the board or on flip charts are legible from the furthest seat in the room. Students unfamiliar with cursive writing styles find printed notes easier to follow.

- Distribute lecture notes and handouts with explanations of key concepts and ideas whenever possible. These may be posted to a class website in electronic format for easier access.

- Allow students to tape lectures. If the technology is available, consider podcasting and posting to the class website.

- Word instructions for assignments clearly and provide step-by-step instructions for assigned tasks. Make examples of completed assignments available, so that students have an idea of the format and standard of work expected.

- Use specific and concrete examples to illustrate and reinforce key concepts and ideas. Incorporate examples from contexts familiar to students from diverse backgrounds. Ask students to help with examples.

- When presenting information, use strategies of advanced structuring (presenting an outline of material), coherence (referring briefly to material previously presented), and extension (providing supplemental reading).

Providing Specific Learning and Study Approaches

- Provide students with tips for note-taking, and suggest approaches for studying difficult material. This may help to generate ideas for papers and prepare students for writing exams. Provide tips specific to your discipline. Encourage students to participate in campus workshops that provide additional help with these tasks.

- Encourage students to study together, share their notes, and consult with each other to reinforce comprehension and to clarify course content.

- For each unit, explain the objectives of the course and the major concepts to be covered. This provides students with a 'big picture' of the planned course material and helps students distinguish between the main ideas in the course and additional supporting information.

- Provide a summary of the key points to be covered in a particular class as an outline for student use.

- If the discipline requires the use of specialized terminology, provide students with a list of relevant dictionaries or other reference materials.

- Encourage pre-reading of assigned readings, and reinforce the importance of adequate preparation. Being prepared will make participating in class activities and discussions easier for linguistically diverse students.

- Review material at regular intervals to check for comprehension. Integrate review activities into instructional strategies to link previous concepts with new ideas.

- Use a variety of techniques to review material. In addition to asking students to summarize and present material verbally, encourage them to display the summary in charts or other visuals or to present written summaries to the class.

Providing Greater Opportunities for Classroom Interaction and Participation

- Incorporate the use of cooperative and collaborative strategies into the classroom.

- Encourage participation in the classroom. Provide students with questions to think about to help them prepare for a class, or ask them to come with a written response to an assigned reading. Having a written piece of work from which to speak may encourage linguistically diverse speakers to contribute more often.

- Encourage students to respond to each other's comments and questions.

- Use email or other communication technologies to provide alternative ways for students and the instructor to communicate. These alternatives can assist students from linguistically diverse backgrounds by giving them more time to think about how to compose a question or response.

Conclusion

In conclusion, we want to emphasize that this Green Guide is not presented to you as a recipe book, nor do we believe there is a recipe book for nurturing cultural diversity in higher education. Any book that provides suggested strategies can run the risk of being adopted without reflection. We ask you not to do this, but rather to utilize these strategies as a way of fostering an environment where both you and your students strive to explore, respect, and become aware of difference, and, as a teacher, to commit yourself to the constant work of challenging assumptions, stereotypes, and inequities in learning environments at every level. Responding to the needs of culturally diverse students requires change at a number of different levels, starting from the self, and moving towards change at the classroom, institutional, and community levels. To implement any of the suggested changes in this guide, we urge you to take into consideration the context in which you teach. Second, to effect changes at all levels, a critical integrative approach, which combines the three selected models and the five dimensions of teaching and learning, is recommended.

Appendix

Culturally Inclusive Teaching – Questions for Instructors

1. Creating a Positive Classroom Environment

Question	Reflection
Am I aware of the diverse backgrounds my students come from and the rich experiences they bring to class?	
Do I try to acknowledge and address these diverse backgrounds and experiences?	
Is the seating arrangement in the classroom welcoming and inclusive?	
Do I demonstrate that class participation is welcomed and encouraged?	
Do I encourage students to express diverse views and opinions and do I model acceptance of this diversity?	
Do I establish clear rules about inappropriate comments (e.g. racist, sexist) or disrespectful behaviour?	
Do I use inclusive language?	
Do I elicit ongoing feedback about the climate in the classroom?	
Am I aware of how my own cultural values and beliefs and possible biases about certain groups of students affect my practice?	

2. Diversifying Curriculum Content

Question	Reflection
Does the curriculum content recognize the different systems of knowledge of diverse groups?	
In my curriculum, do I include or refer to the contributions of people from culturally and linguistically diverse groups?	
Do I select course materials and content which reflect a plurality of views and opinions?	
Do I encourage and challenge students to consider diverse viewpoints, especially those that are different from what is presented as the norm?	
Do I ensure that students understand the social and cultural context in which diverse viewpoints have developed?	
Do I encourage students to question their unexamined assumptions about minority or non-dominant groups?	
Do I provide additional reading to respond to the variety of interests and experiences in the classroom?	

3. Inclusive Instructional Strategies

Question	Reflection
Do I focus on creating a sense of rapport in the classroom to encourage student participation, particularly for those who are new to Canada?	
Are the classroom activities designed to respect and encourage diversity and maximize participation?	
Do I use small and large group discussions effectively?	
Do I use a variety of questioning techniques to elicit responses from different groups of students?	
After asking a question, do I provide sufficient wait time to encourage students to respond, particularly for those who speak English as an additional language?	
Do I acknowledge and validate student participation by building on the contribution of students to class discussion?	
Do I use a variety of strategies and instructional activities to respond to different learning styles?	
Do I provide some choice in the type of assignments students are required to submit?	

4. Assessment Strategies

Question	Reflection
Do I check that students have the knowledge and skills to complete the required assignments?	
Do I provide clear instructions and clarify the expectations for completion of assignments?	
Do I provide a model of a good assignment where possible?	
Am I clear about the criteria for grading assignments?	
Do I make clear connections between course content and the content of the assignment?	
Is there a good balance between individual assignments and group or collaborative assignments?	
If class participation is graded, do I consider the different ways in which students may choose to participate?	
Do I consider using non-traditional methods of assessment (e.g. reading logs, insight cards, visual presentations, community projects)?	

References

Adams, M. (1992). Cultural inclusion in the American college classroom. In L. L. B. Border & N. V. Chism (Eds.), Teaching for diversity. *New Directions for Teaching and Learning, 49*, 5-17. San Francisco: Jossey-Bass.

Anderson, J. A., & Adams, M. (1992). Acknowledging the learning styles of diverse student populations: Implications for instructional design. In L. L. B. Border & N. V. Chism (Eds.), Teaching for diversity. *New Directions for Teaching and Learning, 49*, 19-33. San Francisco: Jossey-Bass.

Association of Universities and Colleges of Canada (AUCC). (2002). *Trends in higher education.* Ottawa: AUCC.

Banks, C. A. M. (2005). *Improving multicultural education: Lessons from the intergroup education movement.* New York: Teachers College Press.

Banks, J. A. (1997a). Multicultural education: Characteristics and goals. In J. A. Banks & C. A. M. Banks (Eds.), *Multicultural education: Issues and perspectives* (5th ed., pp. 3-30). Boston: Allyn and Bacon.

Banks, J. A. (1997b). Approaches to multicultural curricular reform. In J. A. Banks & C. A. M. Banks (Eds.), *Multicultural education: Issues and perspectives* (5th ed., pp. 242-264). Boston: Allyn and Bacon.

Bates, A., & Poole, G. (2003). *Effective teaching with technology in higher education: Foundations for success.* San Francisco: Jossey-Bass.

Benick, G., Newby, D., & Samuel, M. (1996). Forging the links amongst institutional players. In G. Benick & A. Saloojee (Eds.), *Creating inclusive post-secondary learning environments* (pp. 19-34). A project of the Anti-harassment and Discrimination Project Coordination Committee, Ontario Council of Regents and Ontario Council on University Affairs.

Bennett, C. (2001). Genres of research in multicultural education. *Review of Educational Research, 71*(2), 171–217.

Bennett, C. (2003). *Comprehensive multicultural education: Theory and practice* (5th ed.). Boston: Pearson Education.

Bullen, M. (1997). Participation and critical thinking in online university distance education. *Journal of Distance Education, 13*(2), 1-32.

Cabrera, A. F., Crissman, J. L., Bernal, E. M., Nora, A., Terenzini, P. T., & Pascarella, E. T. (2002). Collaborative learning: Its impact on college students' development and diversity. *Journal of College Student Development, 43*(2), 20-34.

Castaneda, C. R. (2004). *Teaching and learning in diverse classrooms.* New York: Routledge Falmer.

Chávez, A. F., Guido-DiBrito, F., & Mallory, S. L. (2003). Learning to value the "other": A framework of individual diversity development. *Journal of College Student Development, 44*(4), 453-469.

Chesler, M. (2002). Effective multicultural teaching in research universities. In J. Chin, C. W. Berheide, & D. Rome (Eds.), *Included in sociology: Learning climates that cultivate racial diversity* (pp. 26-51). Washington, D.C.: National Communication Association & American Association of Higher Education.

Claxton, G., Pollard, A., & Sutherland, R. (2003). Fishing in the fog: Conceptualising learning at the confluence of cultures. In R. Sutherland, G. Claxton, & A. Pollard (Eds), *Learning and teaching where worldviews meet* (pp.1-18). Stoke-on-Trent, UK: Trentham Books.

Coffield, F., Moseley, D., Hall, E., & Kathryn, E. (2004). *Should we be using learning styles? What research has to say to practice.* Learning and Skills Research Centre. Retrieved February 1, 2005, from http://www.lsda.org.uk/pubs/dbaseout/download.asp?code=1540

Cuseo, J. (n.d.). *Cooperative/collaborative structures explicitly designed to promote positive interdependence among group members.* Center for Teaching, Learning and Technology, Illinois State University. Retrieved April 24, 2007, from http://www.ctlt.ilstu.edu/additional/tips/coopStruct.php

Cuseo, J. B. (n.d.). *Capitalizing on student diversity to promote deeper learning and greater appreciation of individual differences: Research-based teaching strategies for college faculty.* Retrieved April 30, 2007, from http://www.geocities.com/deheky/fyejcd.html

Davis, B. G. (1993). *Tools for teaching.* San Francisco: Jossey-Bass.

Dei, G. J. S., James, I. M., Karumanchery, L. L., James-Wilson, S., & Zine, J. (2000). *Removing the margins: The challenges and possibilities of inclusive schooling.* Toronto: Canadian Scholars' Press.

Dei, G. J. S., James-Wilson, S., & Zine, J. (2001). *Inclusive schooling: A teacher's companion to removing the margins.* Toronto: Canadian Scholars' Press.

Dewiyanti, S., Brand-Gruwel, S., & Jochems, W. (2005). Applying reflection and moderation in an asynchronous computer-supported collaborative learning environment in campus-based higher education. *British Journal of Educational Technology, 36*(4), 673–676.

Fenwick, T., & Parsons, J. (2000). *The art of evaluation: A handbook for educators and trainers.* Toronto: Thompson Educational.

Fleras, A., & Elliot, J. L. (2003). *Unequal relations: Race and ethnic dynamics in Canada* (4th ed.). Toronto: Prentice Hall.

Gay, G. (2000). *Culturally responsive teaching: Theory, research and practice.* New York: Teachers College Press.

Ghosh, R., & Abdi, A. (2004). *Education and the politics of difference.* Toronto: Canadian Scholars' Press.

Guo, S. (2000). Increasing class participation and communication with WebCT: An interview with Murray Goldberg - President of WebCT Canada. *Tapestry*, Number 1, January 2000.

Guo, S. (2004). China as a contesting ground for ideologies: Examining the social and ideological forces that influence China's educational system. *Canadian Journal of University Continuing Education. 30*(1), 55-77.

Guo, S. (2005). Preparing teachers to face the challenge of diversity and educational technology in Canadian schools. *The Journal of Border Educational Research*, 3(1), 29-35.

Jalomo Jr., R. (2000). Assessing minority student performance. In S. R. Aragon (Ed.), Beyond access: Methods and models for increasing retention and learning success among minority students. *New Directions for Community Colleges, 112,* 7-18.

Jones, E. B. (2004). Culturally relevant strategies for the classroom. In A. M. Johns & M. K. Sipp (Eds.), *Diversity in college classrooms: Practices for today's campuses* (pp. 51-72). Ann Arbor: University of Michigan Press.

Kees, N. (2003). Creating safe learning environments. In W. M. Timpson, S. S. Canetto, E. A. Borrayo, & R. Yang (Eds.), *Teaching diversity: Challenges and complexities, identities and integrity* (pp. 55-64). Madison: Atwood.

Kinsella, K. (1997). Creating an enabling learning environment for non-native speakers of English. In A. I. Morey & M. K. Kitano (Eds.), *Multicultural course transformation in higher education: A broader truth* (pp. 104-125). Boston: Allyn and Bacon.

Kitano, M. K. (1997a). A rationale and framework for course change. In A. I. Morey & M. K. Kitano (Eds.), *Multicultural course transformation in higher education: A broader truth* (pp. 1-17). Boston: Allyn and Bacon.

Kitano, M. K. (1997b). What a course will look like after multicultural change. In A. I. Morey & M. K. Kitano (Eds.), *Multicultural course transformation in higher education: A broader truth* (pp. 18-34). Boston: Allyn and Bacon.

Ladson-Billings, G. (1992). Culturally relevant teaching: The key to making multicultural education work. In C. A. Grant (Ed.), *Research and multicultural education: From the margins to the mainstream* (pp. 106-121). London: The Falmer Press.

Marchesani, L. S., & Adams, M. (1992). Dynamics of diversity in the teaching-learning process: A faculty development model for analysis and action. In M. Adams (Ed.), Promoting diversity in college classrooms: Innovative responses for the curriculum, faculty, and institutions. *New Directions in Teaching and Learning, 52,* 9-20. San Francisco: Jossey-Bass.

Marshall, P. (2002). *Cultural diversity in our schools.* Belmont: Thomson Learning.

McLaren, P. (2003). *Life in schools: An introduction to critical pedagogy in the foundations of education* (4th ed.). New York: Allyn and Bacon.

Naeth, M. A. (1993). *Teaching resource manual.* Edmonton: University Teaching Services, University of Alberta.

Organization for Economic Co-operation and Development (OECD). (2003). *Trends in international migration: Annual report 2003 edition*. Paris: OECD.

Otten, M. (2003). Intercultural learning and diversity in higher education. *Journal of Studies in International Education, 7*(1), 12-26.

Palmer, P. J. (1998). *The courage to teach: Exploring the inner landscape of a teacher's life*. San Francisco: Jossey-Bass.

Panitz, T., & Panitz, P. (1998). Encouraging the use of collaborative learning in higher education. Retrieved January 17, 2005, from http://home.capecod.net/~tpanitz/tedsarticles/encouragingcl. htm

Sadker, M., & Sadker, D. (1992). Equitable participation in college classes. In L. L. B. Border & N. V. Chism (Eds.), Teaching for Diversity. *New Directions for Teaching and Learning, 49*, 49-55. San Francisco: Jossey-Bass.

Solomon, R. P., & Levine-Rasky, C. (2003). *Teaching for equity and diversity: Research to practice*. Toronto: Canadian Scholars' Press.

Statistics Canada. (2003a). *2001 census: Analysis series*. Ottawa: Statistics Canada.

Statistics Canada. (2003b). *Ethnic diversity survey*. Ottawa: Statistics Canada.

Tisdell, E. J. (1995). *Creating inclusive adult learning environments: Insights from multicultural education and feminist pedagogy* (Information Series No. 361). Columbus, OH: ERIC Clearinghouse on Adult, Career, and Vocational Education, Center on Education and Training for Employment, The Ohio State University.

Vasques-Scalera, C. (2002). The diversity framework informing this volume. In J. Chin, C. W. Berheide, & D. Rome (Eds.), *Included in sociology: Learning climates that cultivate racial diversity* (pp. vii-x). Washington, D.C.: National Communication Association & American Association of Higher Education.

Venable, C. F. (2004). Collaborative learning in the diverse classroom. In A. M. Johns & M. K. Sipp (Eds.), *Diversity in college classrooms: Practices for today's campuses* (pp. 96-113). Ann Arbor: University of Michigan Press.

Wang, M., & Folger, T. (2004). Faculty and student diversity: A case study. In A. M. Johns & M. K. Sipp (Eds.), *Diversity in college classrooms: Practices for today's campuses* (pp. 152-173). Ann Arbor: University of Michigan Press.

Wlodkowski, R. J., & Ginsberg, M. B. (1995). *Diversity and motivation: Culturally responsive teaching.* San Francisco: Jossey-Bass.

Woodward, K. (1997). Concepts of identity and difference. In K. Woodward (Ed.), *Identity and difference.* London: Sage Publications.

About STLHE

A message from Joy Mighty, President

The Society for Teaching and Learning in Higher Education (STLHE) is a national association of academics committed to the improvement of teaching and learning in higher education. STLHE has four primary strategic directions:

1. Advancing the scholarship of teaching and learning.

2. Advocating for excellence in teaching and learning.

3. Achieving inclusivity in all our activities.

4. Alliances—supporting the formation of strategic partnerships.

In pursuit of these four strategic directions, the Society presents an annual conference hosted by a different Canadian institution each year. The conference is renowned for its practical and interactive approach. Attendees include university and college administrators, faculty, educational developers, and students.

The STLHE is a proud sponsor of three unique national awards for excellence in teaching, leadership, collaboration, and achievement. These three awards include:

1. 3M National Teaching Fellowships for teaching excellence and educational leadership—Canada's premier teaching award sponsored by 3M Canada.

2. The Alan Blizzard Award for collaboration in teaching—sponsored by McGraw-Hill Ryerson.

3. The Christopher Knapper Lifetime Achievement Award representing significant contributions to teaching, learning, and educational development in Canadian higher education—sponsored by Magna Publications.

In addition, the Society produces the Green Guide Series—publications which address the most common challenges faculty encounter in their teaching practice.

To keep its members informed, the STLHE produces a tri-annual newsletter *Teaching and Learning in Higher Education*, and hosts an extremely active listserv *Forum for Teaching and Learning in Higher Education*. Listserv members are faculty and educational developers from post-secondary institutions across Canada and beyond.

The STLHE is organized by a Steering Committee—an enthusiastic group of faculty and educational developers who have either been elected by their peers or appointed in recognition of the essential role they play in supporting the Society's work.

Elected positions include a president, past-president, president-elect, and representatives from the following regions:

- Newfoundland, New Brunswick and Prince Edward Island
- Nova Scotia
- Francophone Quebec
- Anglophone Quebec
- Ontario Southwest
- Ontario Northeast
- Ontario Central
- Manitoba and Saskatchewan
- Alberta
- British Columbia

In addition to these elected positions, the Chairs of the Council of 3M National Teaching Fellows and the Educational Developers Caucus—two very important groups that are officially constituted within the Society—serve on the Steering Committee, along with the Awards Coordinator, Chair of the Publications Committee, and the Treasurer.

STLHE Membership

If you are interested in a forum for the exchange of ideas and information on post-secondary teaching and learning, if you believe that teaching is important and that dedication to its improvement should be recognized, if you feel that the road to professional improvement is best walked in the company of enthusiastic peers, then you should join the Society.

Membership is open to anyone who supports the aims of the Society. For more information on individual and institutional memberships, please visit the Society's website www.stlhe.ca or www.sapes.ca

Joy Mighty, President
Director, Centre for Teaching and Learning
Queen's University
B176 Mackintosh-Corry Hall
Kingston, ON K7L 3N6

Ordering Green Guides

To order please contact:

The Book Store at Western
University Community Centre
The University of Western Ontario
London, ON N6A 3K7
Tel: (519) 661-3520
Fax: (519) 661-3673
Email: bkstor@uwo.ca
Web: www.bookstore.uwo.ca